# ROUTLEDGE LIBRARY EDITIONS: GROUP THERAPY

Volume 4

# GROUP PSYCHOTHERAPY FOR STUDENTS AND TEACHERS

# GROUP PSYCHOTHERAPY FOR STUDENTS AND TEACHERS
## A Selected Bibliography, 1946–1979

Compiled by
**JERALD GROBMAN**

LONDON AND NEW YORK

First published in 1981

This edition first published in 2015
by Routledge
27 Church Road, Hove BN3 2FA

and by Routledge
711 Third Avenue, New York, NY 10017

*Routledge is an imprint of the Taylor & Francis Group, an informa business*

© 1981 Jerald Grobman

All rights reserved. No part of this book may be reprinted or reproduced or utilised in any form or by any electronic, mechanical, or other means, now known or hereafter invented, including photocopying and recording, or in any information storage or retrieval system, without permission in writing from the publishers.

*Trademark notice*: Product or corporate names may be trademarks or registered trademarks, and are used only for identification and explanation without intent to infringe.

*British Library Cataloguing in Publication Data*
A catalogue record for this book is available from the British Library

ISBN: 978-1-138-79428-3 (Set)
eISBN: 978-1-315-74758-3 (Set)
ISBN: 978-1-138-79569-3 (Volume 4)
eISBN: 978-1-315-75463-5 (Volume 4)
Pb ISBN: 978-1-138-80188-2 (Volume 4)

**Publisher's Note**
The publisher has gone to great lengths to ensure the quality of this reprint but points out that some imperfections in the original copies may be apparent.

**Disclaimer**
The publisher has made every effort to trace copyright holders and would welcome correspondence from those they have been unable to trace.

# GROUP PSYCHOTHERAPY FOR STUDENTS AND TEACHERS
*A Selected Bibliography, 1946–1979*

*compiled by*
Jerald Grobman, M.D.

GARLAND PUBLISHING, INC. • NEW YORK & LONDON
1981

© 1981 Jerald Grobman
All rights reserved

**Library of Congress Cataloging in Publication Data**

Grobman, Jerald.
   Group psychotherapy for students and teachers.

   (Garland reference library of social science ; v. 102)
   Includes indexes.
   1. Group psychotherapy—Bibliography.  I. Title.
II. Series.  [DNLM: 1. Psychotherapy, Group—Bibliography.  ZWM 430 G873g 1946–79]
Z6664.N5G74  [RC488]    016.61689'15    81-43339
ISBN 0-8240-9291-0                          AACR2

Printed on acid-free, 250-year-life paper
Manufactured in the United States of America

*To Douglas F. Welpton, M.D.*

# CONTENTS

| | |
|---|---|
| Preface | xi |
| 1. Introduction and Overview | 3 |
| 2. Therapeutic Factors in Group Psychotherapy | 3 |
| 3. Group Cohesiveness | 5 |
| 4. Selection and Referral of Patients | 6 |
| 5. Preparation of Patients | 8 |
| 6. Composition and Size of Therapy Groups | 9 |
| 7. Group Dynamics | |
|    A. General Issues | 9 |
|    B. Specific Dynamic Issues and Concepts | 11 |
| 8. Developmental Stages in Therapy Groups | 12 |
| 9. Therapeutic Models | |
|    A. Introduction and Overview | 13 |
|    B. Tavistock | 13 |
|    C. Group Dynamic | 14 |
|    D. Psychoanalytic | 15 |
|    E. Interactional–Interpersonal | 17 |
|    F. Peer Theory | 17 |
|    G. Existential–Experiential | 17 |
|    H. Gestalt | 18 |
|    I. Psychodrama | 18 |
|    J. Transactional Analysis | 19 |
|    K. Behavioral | 19 |
|    L. Systems Theory Applied to Group Psychotherapy | 20 |
|    M. Encounter Groups | 20 |
|    N. T-Groups and the Laboratory Method | 21 |
|    O. Social Work Groups | 22 |
|    P. Didactic Groups | 22 |
| 10. Transference | 23 |
| 11. Countertransference | 24 |
| 12. Use of Dreams | 25 |

13. Scapegoating .......................................... 26
14. Alternate Sessions .................................... 27
15. Working Through ..................................... 27
16. Termination ........................................... 27
17. Fees .................................................. 28
18. Medication ........................................... 28
19. Specific Therapeutic Issues, Goals, and Techniques
    A. Issues ............................................ 29
    B. Goals ............................................. 30
    C. Techniques ....................................... 30
20. Combined Individual and Group Psychotherapy ....... 31
21. Use of Recorders ..................................... 33
22. Co-Therapy .......................................... 33
23. Group Therapy with Patients in Specific Diagnostic Categories
    A. Borderline Patients .............................. 35
    B. Psychotic Patients ............................... 37
    C. Narcissistic Personality Disorders ................ 44
    D. Alcoholic Patients ............................... 45
    E. Suicidal Patients ................................ 45
    F. Schizoid Patients ................................ 46
    G. Character Disorders .............................. 46
    H. Depressed Patients ............................... 47
    I. Neurotic Patients ................................ 47
    J. Phobic Patients .................................. 48
    K. Masochistic Patients ............................. 48
    L. Homosexual Patients .............................. 48
    M. Geriatric Patients ............................... 49
    N. Dying Patients ................................... 49
    O. Retarded Patients ................................ 50
    P. Blind Patients ................................... 50
    Q. Deaf Patients .................................... 50
    R. Sexual Dysfunction ............................... 50
24. Leaderless Groups .................................... 51
25. Couples Groups ....................................... 52
26. Diagnostic Groups .................................... 54
27. Family Group Therapy ................................ 54
28. Time-Limited Groups ................................. 55
29. Crisis Groups ........................................ 56

Contents

30. After Care Groups .................................. 57
31. Group Therapy in Community Psychiatry ............. 58
32. Teaching and Learning Group Psychotherapy
    A. Issues in Learning Group Psychotherapy .......... 58
    B. Supervision of Group Psychotherapy ............. 60
    C. Training Groups ............................... 61
33. Group Relations..................................... 63
34. Group Therapy in a Medical Setting (Including
    Psychosomatic Patients) ............................. 64
35. Groups with Doctors and Medical Students ........... 67
36. Women's Groups .................................. 68
37. Assertiveness Training Groups ...................... 68
38. Groups for Holocaust Survivors ..................... 68
39. In-Patient Groups ................................. 69
40. Large Groups ..................................... 71
41. Activities in Group Therapy ........................ 72
42. Therapeutic Milieu and the Group Process
    A. General Issues and Definitions ................... 73
    B. Therapeutic Milieu vs. Therapeutic Community .... 75
    C. Group Therapy in the Therapeutic Milieu
        i. General Issues ............................. 76
        ii. Large Milieu Groups ....................... 77
        iii. Small Milieu Groups ....................... 78
43. Research and Outcome Studies ..................... 80
44. Group Psychotherapy with Children
    A. General Issues and Overview .................... 81
    B. Young Children................................. 82
    C. Psychotic Children ............................. 82
    D. Activity Group Therapy ........................ 82
    E. Concurrent Group Treatment of Parents and
       Children ...................................... 83
    F. Latency Age Children .......................... 83
    G. Combined Individual and Group Treatment ....... 85
    H. Adolescents ................................... 85
    I. Deprived Children ............................. 88
    J. The Role of Visitors in Children's Groups ......... 89
    K. Parents Groups ................................ 89
Author Index ...........................................91
Subject Index .........................................107

# PREFACE

## I. History and Purposes of the Development of the Bibliography

Five years ago, when I became the Director of Group Psychotherapy Training in the Department of Psychiatry of the Tufts–New England Medical Center, I was charged with the responsibility of developing a training program in psychodynamic psychoanalytically-oriented group psychotherapy. Because all of the mental health programs affiliated with the Tufts Department of Psychiatry were heavily weighted toward psychoanalytically-oriented individual psychotherapy, I needed to both legitimize and stimulate more interest in group psychotherapy. To accomplish these goals, I began by providing careful in-depth clinical supervision for the small number of therapy groups taking place in medical, community, in-patient and out-patient settings. Although I included in each supervision appropriate readings from the group psychotherapy literature, I realized that a comprehensive training program would require more systematic didactic teaching in the theoretical and practical aspects of group psychotherapy.

To supplement my clinical supervisions, I established a weekly literature seminar. Each year, although I used a different textbook, the students (psychiatric residents, social work, psychology, and nursing students) objected to its use. They complained that the book was expensive and generally dealt with patient groups that were much healthier than those groups the students actually led. In addition, since these students devoted only a small part of their overall training experience to group psychotherapy, they felt that the chapters in the textbooks (each of which had to be read completely for continuity) were too lengthy and burdensome for use in a weekly literature seminar.

In order to make the group psychotherapy literature more accessible to my students, I stopped using textbooks and instead began to use articles from journals and only selected chapters from textbooks. Over time, I found that the articles most helpful to students were relatively brief (i.e., they could be read in an hour or two), made one or two salient points, were easily understood, and were relevant to the students' clinical work. This work was invariably with groups of very disturbed patients.

After several years of collecting group psychotherapy articles, I began to organize these articles into topical categories that were relevant to my clinical supervisions and to the categories that I wanted to address in my literature seminar. Shortly after my organizational efforts began, I realized that I had the makings of a very useful bibliography in group psychotherapy. For the past three years I have continued to collect articles and chapters that would enhance both my clinical supervisions and my literature seminar for beginning students in group psychotherapy.

At the urging of many of my group therapy colleagues, I now present this material for publication. In doing so I make no claim for thoroughness or completeness. I am not suggesting that this is the definitive bibliography on group psychotherapy. However, since it does appear to be the most extensive and usefully organized bibliography of its kind for students, teachers and supervisors of group psychotherapy, I believe that its publication at this time will make a meaningful contribution to the field of group psychotherapy.

## II. Selection of the Material for the Bibliography

### A. *Theoretical Framework*

The articles have been selected to acquaint students with the important aspects of psychoanalytic theory and practice as it has been adapted and applied to psychotherapy groups in a wide range of clinical settings. I have included articles dealing with transactional analysis, gestalt therapy, behavior therapy, and psychodrama because I feel students of psychoanalytic group

## Preface

therapy should know something of the basic theory and techniques used in these different modalities. The articles included under these topics are not the result of a careful comparison of all the articles available in each of these fields. They are a selection of articles that students have found valuable as an introduction to these schools of group therapy.

B. *Clinical Emphasis*

Most of the articles in each category have been selected to help students *treat* patients in a therapy group. This does not mean that the articles have only a practical orientation. Whenever possible I selected articles in which theory was integrated and applied to practice. When I felt the topic warranted it, however, I included articles that were more scholarly. For example, Wallace's article "The Development of Freud's Ideas on Social Cohesion" (item 27) is a real addition to our knowledge of group cohesiveness. Occasionally I included articles that were not directly based on clinical work but attempted to amalgamate two different theoretical approaches. Durkin's article "Toward a Common Basis for Group Dynamics" (item 65) attempts to apply concepts from group dynamics research to a therapeutic setting. Students have invariably found this to be a very provocative article.

Because the bibliography's emphasis is on *treating patients* in groups, the large body of literature in the fields of group dynamics, group relations, T-groups, encounter groups, and research on the small group is not extensively represented here. Instead, I have selected articles which students have found helpful as an introduction to theory and practice in these fields. Asch's article "Opinions and Social Pressure" (item 63); Rice's article "Individual, Group and Intergroup Processes" (item 76); Rioch's article "Group Relations: Rationale and Technique" (item 534); Shaffer and Galinsky's chapter "T-Groups and the Laboratory Method" (item 172); and Rogers' article "The Process of the Basic Encounter Group" (item 159) are all examples of these types of articles.

C. *Journal Articles vs. Textbook Chapters*

Because I chose for the bibliography material that was presented in a brief and succinct manner, most of the citations are from journals. When I selected chapters from textbooks, I chose only those chapters that could be read as relatively self-contained units. Many chapters from Yalom's *The Theory and Practice of Group Psychotherapy* are cited because they fit nicely into the topical categories that students have found relevant to their clinical work. Bion's *Experiences in Groups* (item 98) cannot profitably be read as a series of self-contained chapters. However, I chose to include it in the bibliography because of the importance of Bion's theoretical contributions and because the book is available in paperback and easily accessible to students. (Only recently I learned that *Experiences in Groups* is no longer available either in cloth or paperback editions. However, the chapters of the book first appeared in the journal *Human Relations*, Vols. I–IV, between 1948 and 1951.) I have purposely omitted Durkin's *The Group in Depth*; although it is considered by most experienced practitioners of group psychotherapy to be a seminal work in the field, my students have found the chapters in this book too abstract and difficult to apply to their clinical work. Students have consistently found Durkin's views on psychoanalytic group psychotherapy much more relevant and accessible through the many journal articles she has published over the years (see items 3, 65, 95, 109, 156, 158, 185, 187, 647).

### III. Organization of the Bibliography

In the main body of the bibliography the articles and chapters of books are organized into topical categories. Each category includes articles and chapters which present different points of view as well as different aspects of the same topic. Within each category the material is listed chronologically in order to reflect the historical development of ideas and concepts. Works can easily be located also through the author and subject indices.

## IV. Using the Bibliography

The bibliography can be divided into three parts. The first part (sections 1–22) includes topics that would be suitable for a seminar in basic analytic group psychotherapy. Topics in the second part (sections 23–43) include group therapy with special patient populations, group therapy in special settings, special types of group therapy and research and outcome studies in group therapy. The third part (section 44) is a bibliography on group therapy with children. All of the articles can be used to develop specialized and specific literature seminars or to elucidate issues that arise in the clinical supervision of group psychotherapy.

## Acknowledgments

This bibliography would not have been expanded and completed were it not for the continued support and encouragement of my colleagues Anne Alonso and J. Scott Rutan. Preparing the bibliography for wide circulation required meticulous attention to detail and a considerable sacrifice of time in an already demanding schedule. Their conviction of the real value of my efforts was a great help to me when I felt overwhelmed by the organizational aspects of this project.

I wish to thank my many supervisees and students at both the Tufts Mental Health System and the Northeastern Society for Group Psychotherapy. Their eager reading of this material repeatedly demonstrated how useful and necessary a thoughtfully organized and selected bibliography is to serious students of group psychotherapy.

Finally, I would like to thank Madelon Sann Erlichman for her help in editing the final manuscript and Virginia Matthews for her assistance in organizing and typing it.

# GROUP PSYCHOTHERAPY
FOR STUDENTS AND TEACHERS

## 1. INTRODUCTION AND OVERVIEW

1. Committee on History (1971), A Brief History of the American Group Psychotherapy Association 1943-1968. *International Journal of Group Psychotherapy*. 21:406-435.

2. Fried, E. (1971), Basic Concepts in Group Psychotherapy. In: *Comprehensive Group Psychotherapy*, ed. H.I. Kaplan and B.J. Sadock. Baltimore, Md.: Williams & Wilkins, pp. 47-71.

3. Durkin, H.E. (1974), Current Problems of Group Therapy in Historical Context. In: *Group Therapy 1974: An Overview*, ed. L.R. Wolberg and M.D. Aronson. New York: Stratton Intercontinental Medical Book Corp.

4. Shaffer, J., and Galinsky, M. (1974), Historical Introduction and Overview. In: *Models of Group Therapy & Sensitivity Training*. Englewood Cliffs, N.J.: Prentice-Hall, Inc., pp. 1-18.


## 2. THERAPEUTIC FACTORS IN GROUP THERAPY

5. Frank, J., and Ascher, E. (1951), The Corrective Emotional Experience in Group Therapy. *American Journal of Psychiatry*. 108:126-131.

6. Frank, J.D. (1955), Some Values of Conflict in Therapeutic Groups. *Group Psychotherapy*. 8:142-151.

7. Kelman, H. (1963), The Role of the Group in the Induction of Therapeutic Change. *International Journal of Group Psychotherapy*. 13:399-451.

8. Levin, S. (1963), Comparative Observations of Psychoanalytically Oriented Group and Individual Psychotherapy. *American Journal of Orthopsychiatry*. 33:148-160.

9. Hulse, W.C. (1965), Curative Elements in Group Psychotherapy. *Topical Problems of Psychotherapy*. 5:90-101.

10. Arsenian, J., and Semrad, E.V. (1967), Individual and Group Manifestations. *International Journal of Group Psychotherapy*. 17:82-98.

11. Azima, F.J. (1969), Interaction and Insight in Group Psychotherapy: The Case for Insight. *International Journal of Group Psychotherapy*. 19:259-267.

12. O'Hearne, J.J., and Glad, D.D. (1969), The Case for Interaction. *International Journal of Group Psychotherapy*. 19:268-278.

13. Guttmacher, J., and Birk, L. (1971), Group Therapy: What Specific Advantages? *Comprehensive Psychiatry*. 12:546-556.

14. Maxmen, J.S. (1973), Group Therapy as Viewed by Hospitalized Patients. *Archives of General Psychiatry*. 28:404-408.

15. Wolff, H., and Solomon, E. (1973), Individual and Group Psychotherapy: Complementary Growth Experiences. *International Journal of Group Psychotherapy*. 23:177-184.

16. Yalom, I.D. (1975), The Curative Factors in Group Therapy. In: *The Theory and Practice of Group Psychotherapy*. New York: Basic Books, pp. 3-18.

17. Yalom, I.D. (1975), Curative Factors--Overview. In: *The Theory and Practice of Group Psychotherapy*. New York: Basic Books, pp. 70-104.

## 3. GROUP COHESIVENESS

18. Day, M. (Unpublished paper), Achieving Cohesiveness in Therapy Groups.

19. Frank, J. (1957), Some Determinants, Manifestations and Effects of Cohesiveness in Therapy Groups. *International Journal of Group Psychotherapy.* 7:53-63.

20. Yalom, I.D., and Rand, K. (1966), Compatibility and Cohesiveness in Therapy Groups. *Archives of General Psychiatry.* 15:267-275.

21. Cartwright, D. (1968), The Nature of Group Cohesiveness. In: *Group Dynamics: Research & Theory*, ed. D. Cartwright and A. Zander. New York: Harper & Row. Third edition, pp. 91-109.

22. Liberman, R.P. (1971), Reinforcement of Cohesiveness in Group Therapy. *Archives of General Psychiatry.* 25:168-177.

23. Costell, R.M., and Koran, L.M. (1972), Compatibility and Cohesiveness in Group Psychotherapy: A Reevaluation and Extension. *Journal of Nervous and Mental Disease.* 155:99-104.

24. Roether, H.A. (1972), Cohesiveness and Hostility in Group Psychotherapy. *American Journal of Psychiatry.* 128:1014-1017.

25. Krumboltz, J.D., and Potter, B. (1973), Behavioral Techniques for Developing Trust, Cohesiveness and Goal Accomplishment. *Educational Technology.* 13:26-30.

26. Yalom, I.D. (1975), Group Cohesiveness. In: *The Theory and Practice of Group Psychotherapy*. New York: Basic Books, pp. 45-69.

27. Wallace, E.R. (1977), The Development of Freud's Ideas on Social Cohesion. *Psychiatry*. 40:232-241.

28. Grobman, J. (1978), Achieving Cohesiveness in Therapy Groups of Chronically Disturbed Patients. *Group*. 2:141-148.

29. Hurst, A., et al. (1978), Leadership Style Determinants of Cohesiveness in Adolescent Groups. *International Journal of Group Psychotherapy*. 28:263-277.

## 4. SELECTION AND REFERRAL OF PATIENTS

30. Freedman, M.B., and Sweet, B.S. (1954), Some Specific Features of Group Psychotherapy and Their Implications for Selection of Patients. *International Journal of Group Psychotherapy*. 4:355-369.

31. Slavson, S.R. (1955), Criteria for Selection and Rejection of Patients for Various Types of Group Psychotherapy. *International Journal of Group Psychotherapy*. 1:3-30.

32. Leopold, H.S. (1957), Selection of Patients for Group Psychotherapy. *American Journal of Psychotherapy*. 11:634-637.

33. Neighbor, J.E., et al. (1958), An Approach to the Selection of Patients for Group Psychotherapy. *Mental Hygiene*. 42:243-254.

34. Kaplan, S.R., and Roman, M. (1961), Characteristic Responses in Adult Therapy Groups to the Introduction of New Members: A Reflection on Group Process. *International Journal of Group Psychotherapy*. 11:372-381.

35. Leopold, H.S. (1961), The New Member in the Group: Some Specific Aspects of the Literature. *Inter-

national *Journal of Group Psychotherapy.* 11: 367-371.

36. Mullan, H., and Rosenbaum, M. (1962), The Suitability for the Group Experience. In: *Group Psychotherapy: Theory and Practice*, ed. H. Mullan and M. Rosenbaum. New York: Free Press of Glencoe, Macmillan Publishing Co., pp. 93-105.

37. Stein, A. (1963), Indications for Group Psychotherapy and Selection of Patients. *Journal of the Hillside Hospital.* 12:145-155.

38. Heckel, R.V. (1965), Characteristics of Early Dropouts from Group Psychotherapy. *Mental Hygiene.* 49:574-576.

39. Pinney, E.L. (1965), The Psychiatric Indications for Group Psychotherapy. *Psychosomatics.* 6:139-144.

40. Yalom, I.D. (1966), A Study of Group Therapy Dropouts. *Archives of General Psychiatry.* 14:393-414.

41. Grotjahn, M. (1972), Learning from Dropout Patients: A Clinical View of Patients Who Discontinued Group Psychotherapy. *International Journal of Group Psychotherapy.* 22:306-319.

42. Sadoff, R.L. (1973), The Group That Failed. *Psychiatric Quarterly.* 47:110-116.

43. Shafar, S. (1975), Group and Individual Analytic Psychotherapy: Reflections on Four Patients. *Group Analysis.* 9:76-80.

44. Yalom, I.D. (1975), Selection of Patients. In: *The Theory and Practice of Group Psychotherapy.* New York: Basic Books, pp. 219-245.

45. Horwitz, L. (1976), Indications and Contra-Indications for Group Psychotherapy. *Bulletin of the Menninger Clinic.* 40:505-507.

46. Grunebaum, H., and Kates, W. (1977), Whom to Refer for Group Psychotherapy. *American Journal of Psychiatry*. 134:130-133.

## 5. PREPARATION OF PATIENTS

47. Ormont, L. (1957), Preparation of Patients for Group Psychoanalysis. *American Journal of Psychotherapy*. 9:841-848.

48. Mullan, H., and Rosenbaum, M. (1962), The Preparation for Introduction into the Group Experience. In: *Group Psychotherapy: Theory and Practice*, ed. H. Mullan and M. Rosenbaum. New York: Free Press of Glencoe, Macmillan Publishing Co., pp. 107-123.

49. Yalom, I.D., et al. (1967), Preparation of Patients for Group Therapy: A Controlled Study. *Archives of General Psychiatry*. 17:416-427.

50. McGee, T.F. (1969), Comprehensive Preparation for Group Psychotherapy. *American Journal of Psychotherapy*. 23:303-312.

51. Rabin, H.M. (1970), Preparing Patients for Group Psychotherapy. *International Journal of Group Psychotherapy*. 20:135-145.

52. Heitler, J.B. (1973), Preparation of Lower-Class Patients for Expressive Group Psychotherapy. *Journal of Consulting and Clinical Psychology*. 41:251-260.

53. Gauron, E.R., and Rawlings, E.I. (1975), A Procedure for Orienting New Members to Group Psychotherapy. *Small Group Behavior*. 6:293-307.

54. Yalom, I.D. (1975), Composition of Therapy Groups. In: *The Theory and Practice of Group Psychotherapy*. New York: Basic Books, pp. 246-275.

55. Lothenstein, L.M. (1978), The Group Psychotherapy Dropout Phenomenon Revisited. *American Journal of Psychiatry*. 12:1492-1495.

## 6. COMPOSITION AND SIZE OF THERAPY GROUPS

56. Geller, J.J. (1951), Concerning the Size of Therapy Groups. *International Journal of Group Psychotherapy*. 1:1-2.

57. Glatzer, H.T. (1956), The Relative Effectiveness of Clinically Homogeneous and Heterogeneous Psychotherapy Groups. *International Journal of Group Psychotherapy*. 3:258-265.

58. Furst, W. (1960), Homogeneous Versus Heterogeneous Groups. *Topical Problems of Psychotherapy*. 2:170-173.

59. Haythorn, W.W. (1968), The Composition of Groups: A Review of the Literature. *Acta Psychologia*. 28:97-128.

60. Zimet, C.N., and Schneider, C. (1969), Effects of Group Size on Interaction in Small Groups. *Journal of Social Psychology*. 77:177-187.

61. Lindsay, J.S.B. (1972), On the Number in a Group. *Human Relations*. 25:47-64.

## 7. GROUP DYNAMICS

### A. General Issues

62. Foulkes, S.H. (1953), Some Similarities and Differences Between Psychoanalytic and Group Dynamic

Principles. *British Journal of Medical Psychology.* 26:30-35.

63. Asch, S. (1955), Opinions and Social Pressure. *Scientific American.* 193:31-35.

64. Mann, J. (1955), Some Theoretic Concepts of the Group Process. *International Journal of Group Psychotherapy.* 5:235-241.

65. Durkin, H.E. (1957), Toward a Common Basis for Group Dynamics. *International Journal of Group Psychotherapy.* 7:115-130.

66. Slavson, S.R. (1957), Are There Group Dynamics in Therapy Groups? *International Journal of Group Psychotherapy.* 7:131-154.

67. Wolf, A., and Schwartz, E.K. (1960), Psychoanalysis in Groups: The Mystique of Group Dynamics. *Topical Problems in Psychotherapy.* 11:119-154.

68. Stock, D., and Lieberman, M. (1962), Methodological Issues in the Assessment of Total-Group Phenomena in Group Therapy. *International Journal of Group Psychotherapy.* 11:312-325.

69. Parloff, M.B. (1963), Group Dynamics and Group Psychotherapy. *International Journal of Group Psychotherapy.* 13:393-398.

70. Krieger, M.H., and Kogan, W.S. (1964), A Study of Group Processes in the Small Therapeutic Group. *International Journal of Group Psychotherapy.* 14:178-188.

71. Astrachan, B. (1967), The Psychiatrist's Effect on the Behavior and Interaction of Therapy Groups. *American Journal of Psychiatry.* 123:1379-1387.

72. Lieberman, M.A. (1967), The Implications of Total Group Phenomena Analysis for Patients and Therapists *International Journal of Group Psychotherapy.* 17:71-81.

73. Zinberg, N.E., and Friedman, L.J. (1967), Problems in Working Dynamic Groups. *International Journal of Group Psychotherapy*. 17:447-456.

74. Zinberg, N.E., and Glotfelty, J. (1968), The Power of the Peer Group. *International Journal of Group Psychotherapy*. 18:155-164.

75. Lieberman, M.A.; Lakin, M.; and Whitaker, D.S. (1969), Problems and Potential of Psychoanalytic and Group Dynamic Theories for Group Psychotherapy. *International Journal of Group Psychotherapy*. 19:131-141.

76. Rice, A.K. (1969), Individual, Group and Intergroup Processes. *Human Relations*. 22:565-584.

77. Wentworth-Rohr, I. (1969), Origin of the Primary Group: A Contribution to Theory of Groups. *Journal of Group Psychoanalysis and Process*. 2:19-28.

78. Boris, H.N. (1970), The Medium, the Message, and the Good Group Dream. *International Journal of Group Psychotherapy*. 20:91-98.

79. Singer, D.L., et al. (1975), Boundary Management in Psychological Work with Groups. *Journal of Applied Behavioral Science*. 11:137-176.

80. Grunebaum, H., and Solomon, L.F., Toward a Peer Theory of Group Psychotherapy. *International Journal of Group Psychotherapy*. 30:23-50.

B. Specific Dynamic Issues and Concepts

81. Frank, J.D., et al. (1952), Behavioral Patterns in Early Meetings of Therapeutic Groups. *American Journal of Psychiatry*. 108:771-773.

82. Scheidlinger, S. (1964), Identification, the Sense of Belonging and of Identity in Small Groups. *International Journal of Group Psychotherapy*. 14:291-306.

83. Scheidlinger, S. (1966), The Concept of Empathy in Group Psychotherapy. *International Journal of Group Psychotherapy*. 16:413-424.

84. Scheidlinger, S. (1968), The Concept of Regression in Group Psychotherapy. *International Journal of Group Psychotherapy*. 18:3-19.

85. Shader, R.I., and Meltzer, H.Y. (1968), The Breast Metaphore and the Group. *International Journal of Group Psychotherapy*. 18:110-113.

86. Scheidlinger, S. (1974), On the Concept of the "Mother-Group." *International Journal of Group Psychotherapy*. 24:417-428.

87. Grotjahn, M. (1977), The Inroads of Reality into the Therapeutic Group Process. In: *Group Therapy 1977: An Overview*, ed. L.R. Wolberg. New York: Stratton Intercontinental Medical Book Corp., pp. 76-81.

88. Lewis, B.F. (1977), Group Silences. *Small Group Behavior*. 8:109-120.

89. Stone, W.N., and Whitman, R.M. (1977), Contributions of the Psychology of the Self to Group Process and Group Therapy. *International Journal of Group Psychotherapy*. 27:343-359.

## 8. DEVELOPMENTAL STAGES IN THERAPY GROUPS

90. Kaplan, R. (1963), Phases of Development in an Adult Therapy Group. *International Journal of Group Psychotherapy*. 13:10-26.

91. Garland, J.A.; Jones, H.E.; and Kolodny, R.L. (1965), A Model for Stages of Development in Social Work Groups. In: *Explorations in Group Work: Essays in Theory and Practice*, ed. S. Bernstein. Boston: Charles River Books.

## 9. THERAPEUTIC MODELS

### A. Introduction and Overview

92. Hoffman, J.M., and Arsenian, J. (1965), An Examination of Some Models Applied to Group Structure and Process. *International Journal of Group Psychotherapy.* 15:131-153.

93. Bales, R.G. (1970), Perspectives and Theory. *Comparative Group Studies.* 1:315-326.

94. Cohn, R.C. (1970), Therapy in Groups: Psychoanalytic, Experiential, and Gestalt. In: *Gestalt Therapy Now*, ed. J. Fagen and I. Shepard. Science and Behavior Books, pp. 130-139.

95. Durkin, H. (1974), Theoretical Foundations of Group Psychotherapy I. In: *The Challenge for Group Psychotherapy: Present and Future*, ed. S. deSchill. New York: International Universities Press, pp. 1-25.

### B. Tavistock

96. Ezriel, H. (1950), A Psychoanalytic Approach to Group Treatment. *British Journal of Medical Psychology.* 23:59-74.

97. Bion, W.R. (1952), Group Dynamics: A Review. *International Journal of Psychoanalysis.* 33:235-247.

98. Bion, W.R. (1961), *Experiences in Groups.* New York: Basic Books.

99. Ezriel, H. (1967), The First Session in Psychoanalytic Group Treatment. *Nederlands Tydskrift Voor Gemeeskunde.* 111:711-716.

100. Rioch, M. (1970), The Work of Wilfred Bion on Groups. *Psychiatry.* 33:56-66.

101. Ezriel, H. (1973), Psychoanalytic Group Therapy. In: *Group Therapy 1973: An Overview*, ed. L. Wolberg and E.K. Schwartz. New York: Stratton Intercontinental Medical Book Corp., pp. 183-210.

102. Shaffer, J., and Galinsky, M. (1974), The Tavistock Approach to Groups. In: *Models of Group Therapy and Sensitivity Training*. Englewood Cliffs, N.J.: Prentice-Hall, Inc., pp. 164-188.

C. Group Dynamic

103. Whitman, R.M.; Lieberman, M.A.; and Stock, D. (1960), The Relation Between Individual and Group Focal Conflicts. *International Journal of Group Psychotherapy*. 10:259-286.

104. Foulkes, S.H. (1961), Group Processes and the Individual in the Therapeutic Group. *British Journal of Medical Psychology*. 34:23-31.

105. Horwitz, L. (1971), Group Centered Interventions in Therapy Groups. *Comparative Group Studies*. 2:311-331.

106. Shaffer, J., and Galinsky, M. (1974), The Group-Dynamic Therapy Group. In: *Models of Group Therapy and Sensitivity Training*. Englewood Cliffs, N.J.: Prentice-Hall, Inc., pp. 69-89.

107. Borriello, J.F. (1976), Leadership in the Therapist-Centered Group-As-A-Whole Psychotherapy Approach. *International Journal of Group Psychotherapy*. 26:149-162.

108. Horwitz, L. (1977), A Group-Centered Approach to Group Psychotherapy. *International Journal of Group Psychotherapy*. 27:423-439.

## D. Psychoanalytic

109. Durkin, H.E. (1948), The Theory and Practice of Group Psychotherapy. *Annals of the New York Academy of Science.* 51:889-901.

110. Wolf, A. (1949), The Psychoanalysis of Groups. *American Journal of Psychotherapy.* 3:525-558.

111. Berman, L. (1950), Psychoanalysis and Group Psychotherapy. *Psychoanalytic Review.* 37:156-163.

112. Wolf, A. (1950), The Psychoanalysis of Groups. *American Journal of Psychotherapy.* 4:16-50.

113. Powdermaker, F.B. (1951), Psychoanalytic Concepts in Group Psychotherapy. *International Journal of Group Psychotherapy.* 1:16-21.

114. Slavson, S.R. (1951), Dynamics of Analytic Group Therapy. *International Journal of Group Psychotherapy.* 1:208-217.

115. Scheidlinger, S., (1952), Freudian Group Psychology and Group Psychotherapy. *American Journal of Ortho-Psychiatry.* 22:710-717.

116. Slavson, S.R. (1956), Freud's Contributions to Group Psychotherapy. *International Journal of Group Psychotherapy.* 6:349-357.

117. Semrad, E.V.; Kantar, S.; Shapiro, D.; and Arsenian, J. (1963), The Field of Group Psychotherapy. *International Journal of Group Psychotherapy.* 13:452-475.

118. Brockbank, R. (1966), Analytic Group Psychotherapy. In: *Current Psychiatric Therapies*, ed. J.H. Masserman. New York: Grune and Stratton, pp. 145-156.

119. Semrad, E.V., and Day, M. (1966), Group Psychotherapy. *Journal of the American Psychoanalytic Association.* 14:591-618.

120. Parloff, M.B. (1968), Analytic Group Psychotherapy. In: *Modern Psychoanalysis*, ed. J. Marmor. New York: Basic Books.

121. Brockbank, R. (1971), Theory of Therapeutic Rationale in Analytic Group Psychotherapy. *Group Processes*. 4:73-86.

122. Scheidlinger, S. (1971), *Psychoanalysis and Group Behavior: A Study of Freudian Group Psychology*. Westport, Conn.: Greenwood Press.

123. Becker, B.J. (1972), The Psychodynamics of Analytic Group Psychotherapy. *American Journal of Psychoanalysis*. 32:177-185.

124. Freud, S. (1972), *Group Psychology and the Analysis of the Ego*. New York: Liveright.

125. Grotjahn, M. (1973), Selected Clinical Observations from Psychoanalytic Group Psychotherapy. In: *Group Therapy 1973: An Overview*, ed. L.R. Wolberg and E.K. Schwartz. New York: Stratton Intercontinental Medical Book Corp., pp. 43-54.

126. Shaffer, J., and Galinsky, M. (1974), The Psychoanalytic Therapy Group. In: *Models of Group Therapy and Sensitivity Training*. Englewood Cliffs, N.J.: Prentice-Hall, Inc., pp. 49-68.

127. Wolf, A. (1974), Psychoanalysis in Groups: In: *The Challenge for Group Psychotherapy: Present and Future*, ed. S. deSchill. New York: International Universities Press, pp. 120-172.

128. Yalom, I.D. (1974), A Review of Group Psychology and the Analysis of the Ego. *International Journal of Group Psychotherapy*. 24:67-82.

129. Saravay, S.M. (1975), Group Psychology and the Structural Theory: A Revised Psychoanalytic Model of Group Psychology. *Journal of the American Psychoanalytic Association*. 23:69-89.

130. Ammon, G. (1977), Ego-Psychological and Group Dynamic Aspects of Psychoanalytic Group Psychotherapy. In: *Group Therapy 1977: An Overview*, ed. L.R. Wolberg. New York: Stratton Intercontinental Medical Book Corp., pp. 14-26.

131. Wallace, E.R. (1977), The Development of Freud's Ideas on Social Cohesion. *Psychiatry*. 40:232-241.

### E. Interactional-Interpersonal

132. Hidas, G., and Buda, B. (1973), Communication and Aggression in Psychoanalytic Groups: The Group Process from the Viewpoint of Interpersonal Communication Theory. *International Journal of Group Psychotherapy*. 23:148-154.

133. Yalom, I.D. (1975), The Therapist: Tasks and Techniques. In: *The Theory and Practice of Group Psychotherapy*. New York: Basic Books, pp. 105-190.

### F. Peer Theory

134. Grunebaum, H., and Solomon, L. (1980), Toward a Peer Theory of Group Psychotherapy. *International Journal of Group Psychotherapy*. 30:23-50.

### G. Existential-Experiential

135. Shaffer, J., and Galinsky, M. (1974), The Existential-Experiential Therapy Group. In: *Models of Group Therapy and Sensitivity Training*. Englewood Cliffs, N.J.: Prentice-Hall, Inc., pp. 90-107.

136. Mullan, H. (1978), An Existential Group Psychotherapy. *International Journal of Group Psychotherapy*. 28:163-174.

## H. Gestalt

137. Mintz, E.E. (1971), Therapy Techniques and Encounter Techniques: Comparison and Rationale. *American Journal of Psychotherapy*. 25:104-109.

138. Rosen, S., and Kassau, M. (1972), Recent Experiences with Gestalt, Encounter and Hypnotic Techniques. *American Journal of Psychoanalysis*. 32:90-105.

139. Shaffer, J., and Galinsky, M. (1974), The Gestalt Therapy Workshop. In: *Models of Group Therapy and Sensitivity Training*. Englewood Cliffs, N.J.: Prentice-Hall, Inc., pp. 128-147.

140. Gruen, W. (1978), Use of the Leader and of the Group Process in Gestalt Therapy Groups. *Group*. 2:195-209.

## I. Psychodrama

141. Moreno, J.L. (1959), Psychodrama. *American Handbook of Psychiatry*. 2:1375-1396.

142. Solomon, M.D., and Solomon, C.K. (1970), Psychodrama as an Ancillary Therapy on a Psychiatric Ward. *Canadian Psychiatric Association Journal*. 15:365-373.

143. Williams, R.L., and Gasdick, J.M. (1970), Practical Applications of Psychodrama: An Action Therapy for Chronic Patients. *Hospital Community Psychiatry*. 21:187-189.

144. Mintz, E.E. (1974), On the Dramatization of Psychoanalytic Interpretations. In: *Group Therapy 1974: An Overview*, ed. L.R. Wolberg and M.D. Aronson. New York: Stratton Intercontinental Medical Book Corp.

145. Shaffer, J., and Galinsky, M. (1974), Psychodrama. In: *Models of Group Therapy and Sensitivity Training*. Englewood Cliffs, N.J.: Prentice-Hall, Inc., pp. 108-127.

### J. Transactional Analysis

146. Goulding, R., (1976), Four Models of Transactional Analysis. *International Journal of Group Psychotherapy*. 26:385-392.

147. O'Hearne, J.J. (1976), How and Why Do Transactional-Gestalt Therapists Work as They Do? *International Journal of Group Psychotherapy*. 26:163-172.

### K. Behavioral

148. Kaplan, H.I., and Sadock, B.J. (1971), Structured Interaction: A New Technique in Group Psychotherapy. *American Journal of Psychotherapy*. 25:418-427.

149. Liberman, R.P. (1971), Behavioral Group Therapy: A Controlled Study. *British Journal of Psychiatry*. 119:535-544.

150. Birk, L. (1974), Intensive Group Therapy: An Effective Behavioral-Psychoanalytic Method. *American Journal of Psychiatry*. 131:11-16.

151. Shaffer, J., and Galinsky, M. (1974), Behavior Therapy in Groups. In: *Models of Group Therapy and Sensitivity Training*. Englewood Cliffs, N.J.: Prentice-Hall, Inc., pp. 148-163.

152. Heckel, R., and Salzberg, H. (1976), Theoretical Foundations. In: *Group Psychotherapy: A Behavioral Approach*. Columbia, S.C.: University of South Carolina Press, pp. 3-27.

153. Gruen, W. (1977), The Encouragement and Reinforcement of Coping Strengths as a Therapeutic Goal and Strategy in Group Therapy. In: *Group Therapy 1977: An Overview*, ed. L.R. Wolberg and M.D. Aronson. New York: Stratton Intercontinental Medical Book Corp., pp. 239-249.

L. Systems Theory Applied to Group Psychotherapy

154. Astrachan, B.M. (1970), Towards a Social Systems Model of Therapeutic Groups. *Social Psychiatry* 5:110-119.

155. Huskill, E.L. (1973), Toward a Cybernetic Model of Group Therapy. *American Journal of Psychotherapy*. 23:251-264.

156. Durkin, H. (1975), The Development of Systems Theory and its Implications for the Theory and Practice of Group Therapy. In: *Group Therapy 1975: An Overview*, ed. L.R. Wolberg and M.D. Aronson. New York: Stratton Intercontintental Medical Book Corp., pp. 8-20.

157. Ganzarain, R. (1977), General Systems and Object-Relations Theories: Their Usefulness in Group Psychotherapy. *International Journal of Group Psychotherapy*. 27:441-456.

158. Durkin, H. (1978), The Role of the Group Therapist in an Evolving General-Systems Model for Group Psychotherapy. In: *Changing Approaches to the Psychotherapies*, ed. H. Grayson and C. Loew. New York: Spectrum Publications.

M. Encounter Groups

159. Rogers, C. (1967), The Process of the Basic Encounter Group. In: *Challenges of Humanistic Psychology*, ed. J.F.T. Bugental. New York: McGraw-Hill Book Company, pp. 261-276.

160. Casriel, D.H., and Deitch, D. (1968), The Marathon: Time Extended Group Therapy. In: *Current Psychiatric Therapies*, ed. J.H. Masserman. New York: Grune and Stratton, pp. 163-168.

161. Rogers, C. (1969), The Group Comes of Age. *Psychology Today*. 3:27-31.

162. Parloff, M.D. (1970), Group Therapy and the Small Group Field: An Encounter. *International Journal of Group Psychotherapy*. 20:268-304.

163. Yalom, I.D., et al. (1971), A Study of Encounter Group Casualties. *Archives of General Psychiatry*. 25:16-30.

164. Heilfron, M. (1972), Leading Here and Now Groups. *Personal Guidance Journal*. 50:673-678.

165. Geis, H.J. (1973), Effectively Leading a Group in the Present Moment. *Educational Technology*. 13:76-88.

166. Shaffer, J., and Galinsky, M. (1974), The Encounter Group. In: *Models of Group Therapy and Sensitivity Training*. Englewood Cliffs, N.J.: Prentice-Hall, Inc., pp. 211-241.

167. Teicher, A., et al. (1974), Group Psychotherapy and the Intense Group Experience: A Preliminary Rationale for Encounter as a Therapeutic Agent in the Mental Health Field. *International Journal of Group Psychotherapy*. 24:159-173.

168. Yalom, I.D. (1975), Group Therapy and the New Groups. *The Theory and Practice of Group Psychotherapy*. New York: Basic Books, pp. 455-502.

N. T-Groups and the Laboratory Method

169. Gottschalk, L.A., and Pattison, E.M. (1969), Psychiatric Perspectives on T-Groups and the Laboratory

Movement: An Overview. *American Journal of Psychiatry.* 126:823-839.

170. Lubin, B., and Eddy, W. (1970), The Laboratory Training Model: Rationale, Method, and Some Thoughts for the Future. *International Journal of Group Psychotherapy.* 20:305-339.

171. Saretsky, T. (1971), The Application of T-Group Techniques to Ongoing Group Psychotherapy. *Group Process,* 3:57-66.

172. Shaffer, J., and Galinsky, M. (1974), T-Groups and the Laboratory Method. In: *Models of Group Therapy and Sensitivity Training.* Englewood Cliffs, N.J.: Prentice-Hall, Inc., pp. 189-210.

O. Social Work Groups

173. Shaffer, J., and Galinsky, M. (1974), The Social Work Group. In: *Models of Group Therapy and Sensitivity Training.* Englewood Cliffs, N.J.: Prentice-Hall, Inc., pp. 19-48.

P. Didactic Groups

174. Klapman, J.W. (1950), The Case for Didactic Group Psychotherapy. *Diseases of the Nervous System.* 11:35-41.

175. Druck, A.B. (1978), The Role of Didactic Group Psychotherapy in Short-Term Psychiatric Settings. *Group.* 2:98-109.

## 10. TRANSFERENCE

176. Glatzer, H. (1953), Handling Transference Resistance in Group Therapy. *Psychoanalytic Review*. 40:36-43.

177. Demarest, E., and Teicher, A. (1954), Transference in Group Therapy: Its Use by Co-Therapists of Opposite Sexes. *Psychiatry*. 17:187-202.

178. Ezriel, H. (1959), The Role of Transference in Psychoanalysis and Other Approaches to Group Treatment. *ACTA Psychotherapeutica*. 7(supp.): 101-116.

179. Farrell, J.P. (1962), Transference Dynamics of Group Psychotherapy. *Archives of General Psychiatry*. 6:82-92.

180. Belinkoff, J.; Bross, R.; and Stein, A. (1964), The Effect of Group Psychotherapy on Anaclitic Transference. *International Journal of Group Psychotherapy*. 14:474-481.

181. Horwitz, L. (1964), Transference in Training Groups and Therapy Groups. *International Journal of Group Psychotherapy*. 14:202-213.

182. Stein, A. (1964), The Nature of Transference in Combined Therapy. *International Journal of Group Psychotherapy*. 14:413-424.

183. Fried, E. (1965), Some Aspects of Group Dynamics and the Analysis of Transference and Defenses. *International Journal of Group Psychotherapy*. 15:44-56.

184. Glatzer, H. (1965), Aspects of Transference in Group Psychotherapy. *International Journal of Group Psychotherapy*. 15:167-176.

185. Durkin, H.E. (1971), Transference in Group Psychotherapy Revisited. *International Journal of Group Psychotherapy*. 21:11-22.

186. Slavson, S.R. (1972), Group Psychotherapy and the Transference Neurosis. *International Journal of Group Psychotherapy*. 22:422-443.

187. Durkin, H., and Glatzer, H. (1973), Transference Neurosis in Group Psychotherapy: The Concept and the Reality. In: *Group Therapy 1973*, ed. L.R. Wolberg and E.K. Schwartz. New York: Intercontinental Medical Book Corp., pp. 129-144.

188. Yalom, I.D. (1975), The Therapist: Transference and Transparency. In: *The Theory and Practice of Group Psychotherapy*. New York: Basic Books, pp. 191-218.


## 11. COUNTERTRANSFERENCE

189. Goodman, M.; Marks, M.; and Rockberger, H. (1964), Resistance in Group Psychotherapy Enhanced by the Countertransference Reactions of the Therapists. *International Journal of Group Psychotherapy*. 14:332-343.

190. Bernstein, S.; Wacks, J.; and Christ, J. (1969), The Effect of Group Psychotherapy on the Psychotherapist. *American Journal of Psychotherapy*. 23:271-282.

191. Wacks, J., et al. (1970), Some Effects on the Group Psychotherapist in the Group Situation. *Journal of Group Psychoanalysis and Process*. 2:37-44.

192. Neto, B. (1971), Some Aspects of Countertransference in Group Psychotherapy. *International Journal of Group Psychotherapy*. 21:95-98.

193. Ormont, L.R. (1971), The Use of the Objective Countertransference to Resolve Group Resistances. *Group Process*. 3:95-111.

194. Spotnitz, H. (1972), Touch Countertransference in Group Psychotherapy. *International Journal of Group Psychotherapy.* 22:455-463.

195. Weiner, M.F. (1972), Self-Exposure by the Therapist as a Therapeutic Technique. *American Journal of Psychotherapy.* 26:42-51.

196. Dies, R.R. (1973), Group Therapist Self-Disclosure: An Evaluation by Clients. *Journal of Counseling Psychology.* 20:344-348.

197. Kadis, A.L., and Markowitz, M. (1973), Countertransference Between Co-Therapists in a Couples Psychotherapy Group. In: *Group Therapy 1973: An Overview,* ed. L.R. Wolberg and E.K. Schwartz. New York: Intercontinental Medical Book Corp., p. 113.

198. Mintz, E.E. (1978), Group Supervision: An Experiential Approach. *International Journal of Group Psychotherapy.* 28:467-479.

## 12. USE OF DREAMS

199. Klein-Lipshutz, E. (1953), Comparison of Dreams in Individual and Group Psychotherapy. *International Journal of Group Psychotherapy.* 3:143-149.

200. Wolf, A., and Schwartz, E.K. (1962), Dreams. In: *Psychoanalysis in Groups.* New York: Grune and Stratton.

201. Chalfen, L. (1964), Use of Dreams in Psychoanalytic Group Psychotherapy. *Psychoanalytic Review.* 51:461-468.

202. Fielding, B. (1967), Dreams in Group Psychotherapy. *Psychotherapy: Theory, Research and Practice.* 4:74-77.

203. Zimmerman, P. (1967), Some Characteristics of Dreams in Group-Analytic Psychotherapy. *International Journal of Group Psychotherapy*. 17:524-535.

204. Simkin, J.S. (1972), The Use of Dreams in Gestalt Therapy. In: *Progress in Group and Family Therapy*, ed. C.J. Sager and H.S. Kaplan. New York: Bruner/Mazel, 4:95-104.

205. Gold, V.J. (1973), Dreams in Group Therapy: A Review of the Literature. *International Journal of Group Psychotherapy*. 23:394-407.

206. Kaplan, S.R. (1973), The "Group Dream." *International Journal of Group Psychotherapy*. 23:421-431.

207. Kaplan, S.R. (1973), Symposium: Dreams and the Group Setting; Introduction. *International Journal of Group Psychotherapy*. 23:387-393.

208. Whitman, R.M. (1973), Dreams About the Group: An Approach to the Problem of Group Psychotherapy. *International Journal of Group Psychotherapy*. 23:408-420.

209. Battegay, R. (1977), The Group Dream. In: *Group Therapy 1977: An Overview*, ed. L.R. Wolberg and M.D. Aronson. New York: Stratton Intercontinental Medical Book Corp., pp. 27-41.

## 13. SCAPEGOATING

210. Toker, E. (1972), The Scapegoat as an Essential Group Phenomenon. *International Journal of Group Psychotherapy*. 22:320-332.

## 14. ALTERNATE SESSIONS

211. Lindt, H., and Sherman, M.A. (1952), "Social Incognito" in Analytically Oriented Group Psychotherapy. *International Journal of Group Psychotherapy*. 2:209-220.

212. Kadis, A.L. (1956), The Alternate Meeting in Group Psychotherapy. *American Journal of Psychotherapy*. 10:275-291.

## 15. WORKING THROUGH

213. Leopold, H.S. (1959), The Problem of Working Through in Group Psychotherapy. *International Journal of Group Psychotherapy*. 9:287-292.

214. Glatzer, H. (1969), Working Through in Analytic Group Psychotherapy. *International Journal of Group Psychotherapy*. 19:292-306.

215. Papanek, H. (1970), Group Psychotherapy Interminable. *International Journal of Group Psychotherapy*. 20:219-223.

216. Yalom, I.D. (1975), The Advanced Group. In: *The Theory and Practice of Group Psychotherapy*. New York: Basic Books, pp. 332-375.

## 16. TERMINATION

217. Magazu, P.; Golner, J.; and Arsenian, J. (1964), Reactions of a Group of Chronic Psychotic Patients to the Departure of the Group Therapist. *Psychiatric Quarterly*. 38:292-303.

218. Sadoff, R., et al. (1968), On Changing Group Therapists. *Psychiatric Quarterly*. 42:156-166.

219. Zimmerman, D. (1968), Notes on the Reactions of a Therapeutic Group to Termination of Treatment by One of Its Members. *International Journal of Group Psychotherapy*. 18:86-94.

220. McGee, T.F.; Schuman, B.N.; and Racusen, F. (1972), Termination in Group Psychotherapy. *American Journal of Psychotherapy*. 24:521-532.

221. McGee, T.F. (1974), Therapist Termination in Group Psychotherapy. *International Journal of Group Psychotherapy*. 24:3-12.

222. Kauff, P.F. (1977), The Termination Process: Its Relationship to the Separation-Individuation Phase of Development. *International Journal of Group Psychotherapy*. 27:3-18.


17. FEES

223. Kadis, A.L., and Winick, C. (1968), Fees in Group Therapy. *American Journal of Psychotherapy*. 22:60-67.


18. MEDICATION

224. Eisner, B.G. (1964), Notes on the Use of Drugs to Facilitate Group Psychotherapy. *Psychiatric Quarterly*. 38:310-328.

225. Payn, S.B. (1965), Group Methods in the Pharmacotherapy of Chronic Psychotic Patients. *Psychiatric Quarterly*. 39:258-263.

226. Covi, L., et al. (1974), Drugs and Group Psychotherapy in Neurotic Depression. *American Journal of Psychiatry*. 131:210-220.

227. Payn, S.B. (1974), Reaching Chronic Schizophrenic Patients with Group Pharmacotherapy. *International Journal of Group Psychotherapy*. 24:25-31.

## 19. SPECIFIC THERAPEUTIC ISSUES, GOALS, AND TECHNIQUES

### A. Issues

228. Stein, A. (1956), The Superego and Group Interaction in Group Psychotherapy. *Journal of the Hillside Hospital*. 5:495-504.

229. Aronson, M.D. (1964), Acting-Out in Individual and Group Psychotherapy. *Journal of the Hillside Hospital*. 13:43-48.

230. Kanter, S.S., et al. (1964), A Comparison of Oral and Genital Aspects in Group Psychotherapy. *International Journal of Group Psychotherapy*. 14:158-165.

231. Glatzer, H.T. (1967), Neurotic Factors of Voyeurism and Exhibitionism in Group Psychotherapy. *International Journal of Group Psychotherapy*. 17:3-9.

232. Ormont, L.R. (1967), Group Resistance and the Therapeutic Contract. *International Journal of Group Psychotherapy*. 18:147-154.

233. Spotnitz, H. (1968), Psychoanalytic Therapy of Aggression in Groups. In: *Current Psychiatric Therapies*, ed. J.H. Masserman. New York: Grune and Stratton, pp. 149-155.

234. Ormont, L.R. (1969), Acting In and the Therapeutic Contract in Group Psychoanalysis. *International Journal of Group Psychotherapy*. 19:420-432.

235. Guttmacher, J. (1973), The Concept of Character, Character Problems and Group Therapy. *Comprehensive Psychiatry*. 14:513-522.

236. Weisselberger, D. (1973), Acting-Out Behavior in Group Psychotherapy: A Reappraisal. *Groups*. 5:57-61.

237. Fried, E. (1974), Does Woman's New Self-Concept Call for New Approaches in Group Psychotherapy? *International Journal of Group Psychotherapy*. 24:265-272.

238. Danesh, H.B. (1977), The Angry Group. *International Journal of Group Psychotherapy*. 27:59-65.

239. Stone, W.N., and Whitman, R.M. (1977), Contributions of the Psychology of the Self to Group Process and Group Therapy. *International Journal of Group Psychotherapy*. 27:343-359.

B. Goals

240. Fried, E. (1970), Individuation Through Group Psychotherapy. *International Journal of Group Psychotherapy*. 20:450-459.

C. Techniques

241. Lucas, D., and Ludwik, M.S. (1964), Group Psychotherapy with Depressed Patients Incorporating "Mood Music." *American Journal of Psychotherapy*. 18:126-135.

242. Munzer, J. (1964), The Effect on Analytic Therapy Groups of the Experimental Introduction of Special

"Warm-up" Procedures During the First Five Sessions. *International Journal of Group Psychotherapy.* 14:60-71.

243. Foulkes, S.H. (1968), On Interpretation in Group Analysis. *International Journal of Group Psychotherapy.* 18:432-444.

244. Ormont, L.R. (1971), The Use of the Objective Countertransference to Resolve Group Resistances. *Group Process.* 3:95-111.

245. Weiner, M.F. (1971), Levels of Intervention in Group Psychotherapy. *Group Process.* 3:67-81.

246. Fried, E. (1972), The Use of Action and Confrontation. *Psychiatric Annals.* 2:40-47.

247. Grayson, H. (1972), The Psychoanalytic Use of Encounter Techniques. *Psychiatric Annals.* 2:16-31.

248. Yalom, I.D., et al. (1975), The Written Summary as a Group Psychotherapy Technique. *Archives of General Psychiatry.* 32:605-613.

249. Yalom, I.D., et al. (1977), The Impact of a Weekend Group Experience on Individual Therapy. *Archives of General Psychiatry.* 34:399-415.

## 20. COMBINED INDIVIDUAL AND GROUP PSYCHOTHERAPY

250. Fried, E. (1954), The Effect of Combined Therapy on the Productivity of Patients. *International Journal of Group Psychotherapy.* 4:42-55.

251. Papanek, H. (1954), Combined Group and Individual Therapy in Private Practice. *American Journal of Psychotherapy.* 8:679-686.

252. Fried, E. (1955), Combined Group and Individual Therapy with Passive Narcissistic Patients. *International Journal of Group Psychotherapy.* 5:194-203.

253. Jackson, J., and Grotjahn, M. (1958), The Treatment of Oral Defenses by Combined Individual and Group Psychotherapy. *International Journal of Group Psychotherapy.* 8:373-382.

254. Sager, C. (1959), The Effects of Group Psychotherapy on Individual Psychoanalysis. *International Journal of Group Psychotherapy.* 9:403-419.

255. Beran, M. (1961), Combined Individual and Group Therapy within a Hospital Team Set-Up. *International Journal of Group Psychotherapy.* 11:313-318.

256. Graham, F. (1964), A Case Treated by Psychoanalysis and Analytic Group Psychotherapy. *International Journal of Group Psychotherapy.* 14:267-290.

257. Mintz, E.E. (1966), Overt Male Homosexuals in Combined Group and Individual Treatment. *Journal of Consulting Psychology.* 30:193-198.

258. Roth, S. (1971), The Shared Patient: Separate Therapists for Group and Individual Psychotherapy. *International Journal of Group Psychotherapy.* 21:44-52.

259. Battegay, R. (1972), Individual Psychotherapy and Group Psychotherapy as Single Treatment Methods and in Combination. *ACTA Psychiat. Scand.* 48:43-48.

260. Wong, N. (1979), Clinical Considerations in Group Treatment of Narcissistic Disorders. *International Journal of Group Psychotherapy.* 29:325-345.

## 21. USE OF RECORDERS

261. Limentani, D.; Geller, M.; and Day, M. (1960), Group Leader-Recorder Relationship in a State Hospital: A Learning Tool. *International Journal of Group Psychotherapy.* 10:333-345.

262. Krasner, J., et al. (1964), Observing the Observers. *International Journal of Group Psychotherapy.* 14:214-217.

263. Bernardez, T. (1969), The Role of the Observer in Group Psychotherapy. *International Journal of Group Psychotherapy.* 19:234-239.

264. Bloom, V., and Dobie, S.I. (1969), The Effect of Observers on the Process of Group Therapy. *International Journal of Group Psychotherapy.* 19:79-87.

265. Dupont, M., et al. (1975), The Observer in the Analytic Psychotherapy Group. In: *Group Therapy 1975: An Overview*, ed. M.D. Aronson and L.R. Wolberg. New York: Stratton Intercontinental Medical Book Corp., pp. 187-200.

266. Stone, W.N. (1975), Dynamics of the Recorder-Observer in Group Psychotherapy. *Comprehensive Psychiatry.* 16:49-54.


## 22. CO-THERAPY

267. Demarest, E., and Teicher, A. (1954), Transference in Group Therapy: Its Use by Co-Therapists of Opposite Sexes. *Psychiatry.* 17:187-202.

268. Kassoff, A. (1958), Advantages of Multiple Therapists in a Group of Severely Acting Out Adolescent Boys. *International Journal of Group Psychotherapy.* 8:70-75.

269. Gans, R.W. (1962), Group Co-Therapists in the Therapeutic Situation: A Critical Evaluation. *International Journal of Group Psychotherapy*. 12:82-88.

270. Mintz, E. (1963), Special Values of Co-Therapists in Group Psychotherapy. *International Journal of Group Psychotherapy*. 13:127-132.

271. MacLennan, B.W. (1965), Co-Therapy. *International Journal of Group Psychotherapy*. 15:154-165.

272. Mintz, E. (1965), Male-Female Co-Therapists: Some Values and Some Problems. *American Journal of Psychotherapy*. 19:293-301.

273. Rabin, H.M. (1967), How Does Co-Therapy Compare with Regular Group Therapy? *American Journal of Psychotherapy*. 21:244-255.

274. Heilfron, M. (1969), Co-Therapy: The Relationship Between the Therapists. *International Journal of Group Psychotherapy*. 19:366-381.

275. McGee, T.F., and Schuman, B.N. (1970), The Nature of the Co-Therapy Relationship. *International Journal of Group Psychotherapy*. 20:25-36.

276. Davis, F., and Lohr, N.E. (1971), Special Problems with the Use of Co-Therapists in Group Psychotherapy. *International Journal of Group Psychotherapy*. 21:143-158.

277. Benjamin, S.E. (1972), Co-Therapy: A Growth Experience for Therapists. *International Journal of Group Psychotherapy*. 22:199-209.

278. Kaye, H., and Kew, C.E. (1973), Reactions of an On-Going Therapy Group to the Temporary Introduction of a Co-Therapist. *Dynamic Psychiatry*. 21:231-237.

279. Strauss, J. (1975), Two Face the Group: A Study of the Relationship Between Co-Therapists. In: *Group Therapy 1975: An Overview*, ed. M.D. Aronson and L.R. Wolberg. New York: Stratton Intercontinental Medical Book Corp., pp. 201-210.

280. Mattison, S., and Schechter, S. (1977), Parental Transference Reactions to a Male and Female Co-Therapist in Group Therapy. In: *Group Therapy 1977: An Overview*, ed. L.R. Wolberg. New York: Stratton Intercontinental Medical Book Corp., pp. 195-207.

281. Levine, C.O., and Dang, J.C. (1979), The Group Within the Group: The Dilemma of Co-Therapy. *International Journal of Group Psychotherapy*. 29:175-184.

## 23. GROUP THERAPY WITH PATIENTS IN SPECIFIC DIAGNOSTIC CATEGORIES

### A. Borderline Patients

282. Hora, T. (1957), Group Psychotherapy in the Rehabilitation Process of the Borderline Patient. *International Journal of Group Psychotherapy*. 7:406-413.

283. Shaskan, D.A. (1957), Treatment of a Borderline Case with Group Analytically Oriented Psychotherapy. *Journal of Forensic Sciences*. 2:195-202.

284. Spotnitz, H. (1957), The Borderline Schizophrenic in Group Psychotherapy. *International Journal of Group Psychotherapy*. 7:155-174.

285. Feldberg, T. (1958), Treatment of Borderline Psychotics in Groups of Neurotic Patients. *International Journal of Group Psychotherapy*. 8:76-84.

286. Wolman, B.B. (1960), Group Psychotherapy with Latent Schizophrenics. *International Journal of Group Psychotherapy.* 10:301-312.

287. Scheidlinger, S., and Pyrke, M. (1961), Group Therapy of Women with Severe Dependency Problems. *American Journal of Orthopsychiatry.* 31:776-785.

288. Goodson, M.D. (1964), Group Therapy with Regressed Patients. *Perspective in Psychiatric Care.* 2:23-31.

289. Mally, M., and Ogston, W. (1964), Treatment of the Untreatables. *International Journal of Group Psychotherapy.* 14:369-374.

290. Pines, M. (1975), Group Therapy with "Difficult" Patients. In: *Group Therapy 1975: An Overview*, ed. M.L. Aronson and L.R. Wolberg. New York: Stratton Intercontinental Medical Book Corp., pp. 102-119.

291. Horwitz, L. (1977), Group Psychotherapy of the Borderline Patient. In: *Borderline Personality Disorders*, ed. P. Hartocollis. New York: International Universities Press, pp. 399-422.

292. Peters, C., and Grunebaum, H. (1977), It Could Be Worse: Effective Group Psychotherapy with the Help-Rejecting Complainer. *International Journal of Group Psychotherapy.* 27:471-480.

293. Bogdanoff, M., and Elbaum, P. (1978), Role Lock: Dealing with Monopolizers, Mistrusters, Isolates, Helpful Hannahs, and Other Assorted Characters in Group Psychotherapy. *International Journal of Group Psychotherapy.* 28:247-262.

294. Kibel, H.D. (1978), The Rationale for the Use of Group Psychotherapy for Borderline Patients on a Short-Term Unit. *International Journal of Group Psychotherapy.* 28:339-358.

295. Roth, B.E. (1979), Problems of Early Maintenance and Entry into Group Psychotherapy with Persons Suffering from Borderline and Narcissistic States. *Group.* 3:3-22.

296. Wong, N. (1979), Clinical Considerations in Group Treatment of Narcissistic Disorders. *International Journal of Group Psychotherapy.* 29:325-345.

297. Grobman, J. (1980), The Borderline Patient in Group Psychotherapy: A Case Report. *International Journal of Group Psychotherapy.* 30:299-318.

B. Psychotic Patients

298. Mann, J., and Semrad, E.V. (1948), The Use of Group Therapy in Psychoses. *Journal of Social Casework.* 29:176-181.

299. Semrad, E.V., and Standish, C.T. (1951), Group Psychotherapy with Psychotics. *Journal of Psychiatric Social Work.* 20:143-150.

300. Standish, C.T.; Gurri, J.; Semrad, E.V.; and Day, M. (1952), Some Difficulties in Group Psychotherapy with Psychotics. *American Journal of Psychiatry.* 109:283-286.

301. Greenbaum, H. (1957), Combined Psychoanalytic Therapy with Negative Therapeutic Reactions. In: *Schizophrenia and Analytic Office Practice*, ed. A.H. Rifkin. New York: Grune and Stratton, pp. 56-65.

302. Kirby, K., and Priestman, S. (1957), Values of a Daughter (Schizophrenic) and Mother Therapy Group. *International Journal of Group Psychotherapy.* 7:281-288.

303. Kramer, H. (1957), Group Psychotherapy with Psychotic Patients. *Journal of Nervous and Mental Disorders.* 125:36-43.

304. Beard, J., et al. (1958), The Effectiveness of Activity Group Therapy with Chronically Regressed Adult Schizophrenics. *International Journal of Group Psychotherapy*. 8:123-136.

305. Hora, T. (1958), The Schizophrenic Patient in the Therapy Group. *Journal of the Hillside Hospital*. 7:110-115.

306. Hulse, W.C. (1958), Psychotherapy with Ambulatory Schizophrenic Patients in Mixed Analytic Groups. *AMA Archives of Neurology and Psychiatry*. 79:681-687.

307. Daniels, R., and Kramer, M. (1959), A Group Psychotherapeutic Program for Chronic Psychotics. *Psychiatric Quarterly*. 3(supp.):119-127.

308. Haley, J. (1959), An Interactional Description of Schizophrenia. *Psychiatry*. 22:321-332.

309. King, C.H. (1959), Activity Group Therapy with a Schizophrenic Boy: Follow-up Two Years Later. *International Journal of Group Psychotherapy*. 9:184-194.

310. Illing, H., and Brownfield, B. (1960), Delusions of Schizophrenic Patients in Group Psychotherapy. *Journal of Social Therapy*. 6:35-43.

311. Beran, M. (1961), Combined Individual and Group Therapy Within a Hospital Team Set-Up. *International Journal of Group Psychotherapy*. 11:313-318.

312. Chesteen, J.E., Jr. (1961), Breaking Through the Resistance in a Group of Psychotic Patients. *International Journal of Group Psychotherapy*. 11:462-467.

313. Forer, B. (1961), Group Psychotherapy with Out-Patient Schizophrenics. *International Journal of Group Psychotherapy*. 11:188-195.

314. Slavson, S. (1961), Group Psychotherapy and the Nature of Schizophrenia. *International Journal of Group Psychotherapy*. 11:3-32.

315. MacLeod, J., and Middleman, F. (1962), Wednesday Afternoon Clinic: A Supportive Care Program. *Archives of General Psychiatry*.6:56-65.

316. Glad, D., et al. (1963), Schizophrenic Factor Reactions to Four Group Psychotherapy Methods. *International Journal of Group Psychotherapy*. 13:196-210.

317. Resnik, S. (1963), Experience with a Group of Chronic Psychotics. *British Journal of Medical Psychology*. 36:327-330.

318. Stotsky, B.A., and Zolik, E.S. (1963), Group Psychotherapy with Psychotics: 1921-1963. A Review. *International Journal of Group Psychotherapy*. 13:321-344.

319. Burke, J.L., and Lee, H. (1964), An Acting-Out Patient in a Psychotic Group. *International Journal of Group Psychotherapy*. 14:194-201.

320. Drennen, W., and Wiggins, S. (1964), Manipulation of Verbal Behavior of Chronic Hospital Schizophrenics in a Group Therapy Situation. *International Journal of Group Psychotherapy*. 14:189-193.

321. Geller, J.J. (1964), Group Psychotherapy in the Treatment of the Schizophrenic Syndromes. *Psychiatric Quarterly*. 37:710-732.

322. Magazu, P.; Golner, J.; and Arsenian, J. (1964), Reactions of a Group of Chronic Psychotic Patients to the Departure of the Group Therapist. *Psychiatric Quarterly*. 38:292-303.

323. Sheps, J. (1964), Group Therapy in Schizophrenia. *International Psychiatry Clinics*. 1:911-928.

324. Wong, N. (1964), Out-Patient Group Psychotherapy with Paranoid Schizophrenic Patients. *Psychiatric Quarterly*. 38:665-678.

325. Alikakos, L.C. (1965), Analytical Group Treatment of the Post-Hospital Schizophrenic. *International Journal of Group Psychotherapy*. 15:492-504.

326. Fidler, J.W. (1965), Group Psychotherapy of Psychotics. *American Journal of Orthopsychiatry*. 35:688-694.

327. Kernberg, P.F. (1965), Experiences with Open Groups on a State Hospital Admission Ward. *Bulletin of the Menninger Clinic*. 29:27-34.

328. McGee, T.F., et al. (1965), Conjunctive Use of Psychodrama and Group Psychotherapy in a Group Living Program with Schizophrenic Patients. *Group Psychotherapy*. 18:127-135.

329. Payn, S.B. (1965), Group Methods in the Pharmacotherapy of Chronic Psychotic Patients. *Psychiatric Quarterly*. 39:258-263.

330. Dumont, M.P. (1966), Death of the Leader in a Therapy Group of Schizophrenics. *International Journal of Group Psychotherapy*. 36:209-215.

331. Horowitz, M.J., and Weisberg, P. (1966), Techniques for the Group Psychotherapy of Acute Psychosis. *International Journal of Group Psychotherapy*. 16:42-50.

332. Shattan, S., et al. (1966), Group Treatment of Conditionally Discharged Patients in a Mental Health Clinic. *American Journal of Psychiatry*. 122:789-805.

333. Weich, M.J., and Robbins, E. (1966), Short-Term Group Psychotherapy with Acutely Psychotic Patients. *Psychiatric Quarterly*. 40:80-87.

334. Christmas, J.J. (1967), Sociopsychiatric Treatment of Disadvantaged Psychotic Adults. *American Journal of Orthopsychiatry.* 37:93-100.

335. Christ, J., and Goldstein, S. (1968), Innovative Techniques in Dealing with Psychotic Disorders in the Out-Patient Clinic. *American Journal of Orthopsychiatry.* 38:292-293.

336. Kibel, H.D. (1968), Group Psychotherapy as an Adjunct to Milieu Treatment with Chronic Schizophrenics. *Psychiatric Quarterly.* 42:339-351.

337. Rueveni, U., and Speck, R. (1969), Using Encounter Group Techniques in the Treatment of the Social Network of the Schizophrenic. *International Journal of Group Psychotherapy.* 19:495-500.

338. Kraus, R.F. (1970), The Use of Symbolic Technique in the Group Psychotherapy of Chronic Schizophrenia. *Psychiatric Quarterly.* 44:143-157.

339. Davis, J.A. (1971), Outpatient Group Therapy with Schizophrenic Patients. *Social Casework.* 52:172-178.

340. Lehrer-Carle, I. (1971), Group Music with Schizophrenics. *Journal of Contemporary Psychotherapy.* 2:111-116.

341. Masnik, R., et al. (1971), Coffee and ... A New Way to Treat the Untreatable. *American Journal of Psychiatry.* 128:164-167.

342. McGee, T.F., and Williams, M. (1971), Time-Limited and Time-Unlimited Group Psychotherapy: A Comparison with Schizophrenic Patients. *Comparative Group Studies.* 2:71-84.

343. O'Brien, C., et al. (1972), Group vs. Individual Psychotherapy with Schizophrenics. *Archives of General Psychiatry.* 27:474-478.

344. Cochrane, N. (1973), Some Reflections on the Unsuccessful Treatment of Schizophrenics. *British Journal of Psychiatry*. 123:395-400.

345. Frey, N.C., and Pizzitola, D. (1973), Group Therapy with Schizophrenics. *Social Work*. 18:94-95.

346. Steiner, J. (1973), The Use of Activity as an Adjunct to Group Psychotherapy: I. *Groups*. 5:15-28.

347. Bower, P.F.; Banquer, M.; and Bloomfield, H.H. (1974), Utilization of Nonverbal Exercises in the Group Therapy of Outpatient Chronic Schizophrenics. *International Journal of Group Psychotherapy*. 24:13-24.

348. Claghorn, J., et al. (1974), Group Therapy and Maintenance Treatment of Schizophrenics. *Archives of General Psychiatry*. 31:361-365.

349. Herz, M.I., et al. (1974), Individual vs. Group Aftercare Treatment. *American Journal of Psychiatry*. 131:808-812.

350. Payn, S.B. (1974), Reaching Chronic Schizophrenic Patients with Group Pharmacotherapy. *International Journal of Group Psychotherapy*. 24:25-31.

351. Almond, R. (1975), Issues in Milieu Treatment. *Schizophrenia Bulletin*. 13:12-36.

352. Comstock, B., and Jones, M.N. (1975), Group Therapy as a Treatment Technique for Severely Disturbed Outpatients. *Hospital and Community Psychiatry*. 26:677-679.

353. Gootnick, I. (1975), Transference in Psychotherapy with Schizophrenic Patients. *International Journal of Group Psychotherapy*. 25:379-388.

354. O'Brien, C.D. (1975), Group Therapy for Schizophrenia: A Practical Approach. *Schizophrenia Bulletin*. 13:119-130.

355. Slavinska-Holy, N. (1975), Spatio-Temporal Considerations in Psychoanalytic Group Psychotherapy of Severely Disturbed Patients. In: *Group Therapy 1975. An Overview*, ed. M.L. Aronson and L.R. Wolberg. New York: Stratton Intercontinental Medical Book Corp., pp. 120-126.

356. Strassberg, D., et al. (1975), Self-Disclosure in Group Therapy with Schizophrenics. *Archives of General Psychiatry*. 32:1259-1261.

357. Liberman, R.P. (1976), Behavior Therapy for Schizophrenia. In: *Treatment of Schizophrenia: Progress and Prospects*, ed. D.E. Flinn and L.J. West. New York: Grune & Stratton, pp. 175-206.

358. Lofgren, L.B. (1976), A Process-Oriented Group Approach to Schizophrenia. In: *Treatment of Schizophrenia: Progress and Prospects*, ed. D.E. Flinn and L.J. West. New York: Grune & Stratton, pp. 206-217.

359. Ludwig, A.M. (1976), Group Treatment Methods for Chronic Schizophrenics. In: *Treatment of Schizophrenia: Progress and Prospects*, ed. D.E. Flinn and L.J. West. New York: Grune & Stratton, pp. 149-158.

360. Van Putten, T., and May, P.R.A. (1976), Milieu Therapy of the Schizophrenias. In: *Treatment of Schizophrenia: Progress and Prospects*, ed. D.E. Flinn and L.J. West. New York: Grune & Stratton, pp. 217-243.

361. Beal, D., et al. (1977), Graded Group Procedures for Long Term Regressed Schizophrenics. *Journal of Nervous and Mental Diseases*. 164:102-106.

362. Cory, T., and Page, D. (1977), Follow the Paranoid: A Group Method for Effecting Change in Paranoid Patients. *Voices*. 13:33-38.

363. Aiello, T. (1978), Group Psychotherapy of the Hospitalized Psychotic. (Presented at the 1978 A.G.P.A. Conference, New Orleans, La.)

364. Cory, T.L., and Page, D. (1978), Group Techniques for Effecting Change in the More Disturbed Patient. *Group*. 2:149-155.

365. Steiner, J. (1979), Holistic Group Therapy with Schizophrenic Patients. *International Journal of Group Psychotherapy*. 29:195-210.

C. Narcissistic Personality Disorders

366. Fried, E. (1955), Combined Group and Individual Therapy with Passive Narcissistic Patients. *International Journal of Group Psychotherapy*. 5:194-203.

367. Scheidlinger, S., and Pyrke, M. (1961), Group Therapy of Women with Severe Dependency Problems. *American Journal of Orthopsychiatry*. 31:776-785.

368. Glatzer, H.T. (1962), Handling Narcissistic Problems in Group Psychotherapy. *International Journal of Group Psychotherapy*. 12:448-455.

369. Fried, E. (1971), The Narcissistic Cocoon: How It Curbs and Can Be Curbed. *Group Process*. 4:87-95.

370. Roth, B.E. (1979), Problems of Early Maintenance and Entry into Group Psychotherapy with Persons Suffering from Borderline and Narcissistic States. *Group*. 3:3-22.

371. Wong, N. (1979), Clinical Considerations in Group Treatment of Narcissistic Disorders. *International Journal of Group Psychotherapy*. 29:325-345.

D. Alcoholic Patients

372. Fox, R. (1965), Modifications of Group Psychotherapy for Alcoholics. *American Journal of Orthopsychiatry.* 35:258-259.

373. Curlee, J. (1971), Combined Use of Alcoholics Anonymous and Outpatient Psychotherapy. *Bulletin of the Menninger Clinic.* 35:368-371.

374. Sands, P.M., et al. (1971), Psychotherapeutic Groups for Alcoholics and Relatives in an Outpatient Setting. *International Journal of Group Psychotherapy.* 21:23-33.

375. Bratter, T.E. (1974), Reality Therapy: A Group Psychotherapeutic Approach with Adolescent Alcoholics. *Annals of the New York Academy of Sciences.* 233:104-114.

376. Yalom, I.D. (1974), Group Therapy and Alcoholism. *Annals of the New York Academy of Sciences.* 233:85-103.

377. Dolan, L.P. (1975), Intake Group in the Alcoholism Outpatient Clinic. *Journal of Studies on Alcohol.* 36:996-999.

378. Brown, S., and Yalom, I.D. (1977), Interactional Group Therapy with Alcoholics. *Journal of Studies on Alcohol.* 38:426-456.

379. Intagliata, J. (1979), Increasing the Responsiveness of Alcoholics to Group Therapy: An Interpersonal Problem-Solving Approach. *Group.* 3:106-120.

E. Suicidal Patients

380. Indin, B.M. (1966), The Crisis Club: A Group Experience for Suicidal Patients. *Mental Hygiene.* 50:280-290.

381. Frederick, C.J., and Farberow, N. (1970), Group Psychotherapy with Suicidal Persons: A Comparison with Standard Group Methods. *International Journal of Group Psychotherapy*. 16:103-111.

382. Kibel, H.D. (1973), A Group Member's Suicide: Treating Collective Trauma. *International Journal of Group Psychotherapy*. 23:42-53.

383. Billings, J., et al. (1974), Observations on Long-Term Group Therapy with Suicidal and Depressed Persons. *Suicide and Life Threatening Behavior*. 4:160-170.

384. Comstock, B.S., and McDermott, M. (1975), Group Therapy for Patients Who Attempt Suicide. *International Journal of Group Psychotherapy*. 25:44-49.

F. Schizoid Patients

385. Wermers, D.F., and Wise, M. (1969), A Technique to Integrate the Social Isolate in a Group Activity. *International Journal of Group Psychotherapy*. 19:229-233.

386. Suarez, R. (1970), The Silent Patient in Group Therapy. *Journal of Psychiatric Nursing and Mental Health*. 8:10-12.

G. Character Disorders

387. Crutcher, R. (1961), The Usefulness of Group Therapy with Character Disorders. *International Journal of Group Psychotherapy*. 11:431-439.

388. Vass, I. (1965), The Acting-Out Patient in Group Therapy. *American Journal of Psychotherapy*. 19:302-308.

389. Scheidlinger, S., and Holden, M.A. (1966), Group Therapy of Women with Severe Character Disorders. *International Journal of Group Psychotherapy*. 16:174-189.

390. Rappaport, R.G. (1971), Group Therapy in Prison. *International Journal of Group Psychotherapy*. 21:489-496.

391. Carney, F.L. (1972), Some Recurring Therapeutic Issues in Group Psychotherapy with Criminal Patients. *American Journal of Psychotherapy*. 26:34-41.

### H. Depressed Patients

392. Miller, P.R., and Ferone, L. (1966), Group Psychotherapy with Depressed Women. *American Journal of Psychiatry*. 123:701-703.

### I. Neurotic Patients

393. Powdermaker, F., and Frank, J.D. (1948), Group Psychotherapy with Neurotics. *American Journal of Psychiatry*. 105:449-455.

394. Abroms, G.M., and Kass, D.J. (1972), Behavioral Group Treatment of Hysteria. *Archives of General Psychiatry*. 26:42-50.

395. Glatzer, H.T. (1972), Treatment of Oral Character Neurosis in Group Psychotherapy. In: *Progress in Group and Family Therapy*, ed. C.J. Sager and H.S. Kaplan. New York: Bruner/Mazel, pp. 54-65.

396. Schwartz, E.K. (1972), The Treatment of the Obsessive Patient in the Group Therapy Setting. *American Journal of Psychotherapy*. 26:352-361.

397. Covi, L., et al. (1974), Drugs and Group Psychotherapy in Neurotic Depression. *American Journal of Psychiatry*. 131:191-198.

## J. Phobic Patients

398. Lazarus, A.A. (1961), Group Therapy of Phobic Disorders by Systematic Desensitization. *Journal of Abnormal and Social Psychology*. 63:504-510.

399. Al Salih, H.A. (1969), Phobics in Group Psychotherapy. *International Journal of Group Psychotherapy*. 19:28-34.

## K. Masochistic Patients

400. Glatzer, H.T. (1959), Analysis of Masochism in Group Psychotherapy. *International Journal of Group Psychotherapy*. 9:158-166.

401. Fischer, N., and Crabtree, L.H., Jr. (1969), A Sadomasochistic Struggle in Group Psychotherapy. *American Journal of Psychotherapy*. 23:495-504.

## L. Homosexual Patients

402. Litman, R.E. (1961), Psychotherapy of a Homosexual Man in a Heterosexual Group. *International Journal of Group Psychotherapy*. 11:440-448.

403. Hadden, S. (1966), Group Therapy for Male Homosexuals. In: *Current Psychiatric Therapies*, ed. J.H. Masserman. New York: Grune & Stratton, pp. 177-186.

404. Mintz, E.E. (1966), Overt Male Homosexuals in Combined Group and Individual Treatment. *Journal of Consulting Psychology*. 30:193-198.

405. Nobler, H. (1972), Group Therapy with Male Homosexuals. *Comparative Group Studies*. 3:161-178.

406. Gershman, H. (1975), The Effect of Group Therapy on Compulsive Homosexuality in Men and Women.

*American Journal of Psychoanalysis*. 35:303-312.


## M. Geriatric Patients

407. Liederman, P.C., and Green, R. (1965), Geriatric Outpatient Group Therapy. *Comprehensive Psychiatry*. 6:51-59.

408. Liederman, P.C., et al. (1967), Outpatient Group Therapy with Geriatric Patients. *Geriatrics*. 22:148-153.

409. Burnside, I.M. (1971), Long-Term Group Work with Hospitalized Aged. *Gerontologist*. 11:213-218.

410. Manaster, A. (1972), Therapy with the "Senile" Geriatric Patient. *International Journal of Group Psychotherapy*. 22:250-257.

411. Krasner, J.D. (1974), Analytic Group Psychotherapy with the Aged. In: *The Challenge for Group Psychotherapy: Present and Future*, ed. S. deSchill. New York: International Universities Press, pp. 316-357.


## N. Dying Patients

412. Yalom, I.D., and Greaves, C. (1977), Group Therapy with the Terminally Ill. *American Journal of Psychiatry*. 134:396-400.

413. Spiegal, D., and Yalom, I. (1978), A Support Group for Dying Patients. *International Journal of Group Psychotherapy*. 28:233-245.

O. Retarded Patients

414. Borenzweig, H. (1970), Social Group Work in the Field of Mental Retardation: A Review of the Literature. *Social Service Review*. 44:177-183.

415. Payne, J., and Williams, M. (1971), Practical Aspects of Group Work with the Mentally Retarded. *Group Process*. 4:9-17.

416. Robinson, L.H. (1974), Group Work with Parents of Retarded Adolescents. *American Journal of Psychology*. 28:397-408.

417. Tavormina, J.B. (1975), Relative Effectiveness of Behavioral and Reflective Group Counseling with Parents of Mentally Retarded Children. *Journal of Consulting and Clinical Psychology*. 43:22-31.

P. Blind Patients

418. Herman, S. (1966), Some Observations on Group Therapy with the Blind. *International Journal of Group Psychotherapy*. 16:367-372.

Q. Deaf Patients

419. Robinson, L. (1966), Group Therapy for Deaf Psychiatric Patients. In: *Current Psychiatric Therapies*, ed. J.H. Masserman. New York: Grune & Stratton, pp. 172-176.

R. Sexual Dysfunction

420. Hadden, S.B. (1968), Group Psychotherapy for Sexual Maladjustments. *American Journal of Psychiatry*. 125:327-332.

421. Resnik, H.L.P., and Peters, J.J. (1968), Group Psychotherapy with Sexual Offenders. In: *Current Psychiatric Therapies*, ed. J.H. Masserman. New York: Grune & Stratton, pp. 156-162.

422. Illing, H.A., and Miles, J.E. (1969), Outpatient Group Psychotherapy with Sex Offenders. *International Journal of Social Psychiatry*. 15:258-263.

423. Mickow, G., and Benson, M. (1973), Group Therapy for Sex Offenders. *Social Work*. 18:98-100.

## 24. LEADERLESS GROUPS

424. Bion, W.R. (1946), The Leaderless Group Project. *Bulletin of the Menninger Clinic*. 10:77-81.

425. Astrachan, B.M., et al. (1967), The Unled Patient Group as a Therapeutic Tool. *International Journal of Group Psychotherapy*. 17:178-191.

426. Klein, F.M. (1972), Dynamics of a Leaderless Group. *International Journal of Group Psychotherapy*. 22:234-242.

427. Desmond, R., and Seligman, M. (1975), The Leaderless Group Phenomenon: A Historical Perspective. *International Journal of Group Psychotherapy*. 25:277-290.

428. Hunt, W., and Issacharoff, A. (1975), History and Analysis of a Leaderless Group of Professional Therapists. *American Journal of Psychiatry*. 132:1164-1167.

## 25. COUPLES GROUPS

429. Kirby, K., and Priestman, S. (1957), Values of a Daughter (Schizophrenic) and Mother Therapy Group. *International Journal of Group Psychotherapy*. 7:281-288.

430. Westman, J.C., et al. (1965), A Comparison of Married Couples in the Same and Separate Therapy Groups. *International Journal of Group Psychotherapy*. 15:374-381.

431. Gottlieb, A., and Pattison, E.M. (1966), Married Couples Group Psychotherapy. *Archives of General Psychiatry*. 14:143-152.

432. Blinder, M.G., and Kirschenbaum, M. (1967), The Technique of Married Couple Group Therapy. *Archives of General Psychiatry*. 17:44-52.

433. Jones, W.L. (1967), The Villain and the Victim: Group Therapy for Married Couples. *American Journal of Psychiatry*. 124:351-354.

434. Everett, H.C. (1968), The "Adversary" System in Married Couples Group Therapy. *International Journal of Group Psychotherapy*. 18:70-74.

435. Grunebaum, H., and Christ, J. (1968), Interpretation and the Task of the Therapist with Couples and Families. *International Journal of Group Psychotherapy*. 18:495-503.

436. Grunebaum, H., et al. (1969), Diagnosis and Treatment Planning for Couples. *International Journal of Group Psychotherapy*. 19:185-201.

437. Reckless, J. (1969), A Confrontation Technique Used with Married Couples in a Group Therapy Setting. *International Journal of Group Psychotherapy*. 19:203-213.

438. Kohn, R. (1971), Treatment of Married Couples in a Group. *Group Process.* 4:96-105.

439. Kadis, A.L., and Markowitz, M. (1972), Short-Term Analytic Treatment of Married Couples in a Group by a Therapist Couple. In: *Progress in Group and Family Therapy*, ed. H.S. Kaplan and C.J. Sager. New York: Brunner/Mazel.

440. Cochrane, N. (1973), Some Reflections on the Unsuccessful Treatment of a Group of Married Couples. *British Journal of Psychiatry.* 123:395-401.

441. Leichter, E. (1973), Treatment of Married Couples Groups. *Family Coordinator.* 22:31-41.

442. Gurman, A.S. (1975), Evaluating the Outcomes of Couples Groups. In: *Couples in Conflict*, ed. A. Gurman and D. Rice. New York: Aronson, pp. 192-206.

443. Kilgo, R.D. (1975), Counseling Couples in Groups: Rationale and Methodology. *Family Coordinator.* 24:337-342.

444. Leichter, E. (1975), Treatment of Married Couples Groups. In: *Couples in Conflict*, ed. A. Gurman and D. Rice. New York: Aronson, pp. 175-191.

445. Low, M., and Low, P. (1975), Treatment of Married Couples in a Group Run by a Husband and Wife. *International Journal of Group Psychotherapy.* 25:54-66.

446. Morris, J.D., and Prescott, M.R. (1975), Transition Groups: An Approach to Dealing with Post-Partnership Anguish. *Family Coordinator.* 24:325-330.

447. Spitz, H.I. (1978), Structured Interactional Group Psychotherapy with Couples. *International Journal of Group Psychotherapy.* 28:401-414.

## 26. DIAGNOSTIC GROUPS

448. Peck, H.B. (1953), An Application of Group Therapy to the Intake Process. *American Journal of Orthopsychiatry.* 23:338-349.

449. Stone, A.R.; Parloff, M.D.; and Frank, J.D. (1954), The Use of Diagnostic Groups in a Group Therapy Program. *International Journal of Group Psychotherapy.* 4:274-284.

450. Abrahams, D., and Enright, J.D. (1965), Psychiatric Intake in Groups: A Pilot Study of Procedures, Problems and Prospects. *American Journal of Psychiatry.* 122:170-174.

451. McGee, T.F., and Larson, V.B. (1967), An Approach to Waiting List Therapy Groups. *American Journal of Orthopsychiatry.* 37:594-597.

452. Chiles, J.A., et al. (1972), Group Intake, Brief Therapy and the Use of Expertise: Evolving Changes in Intake Procedure. *Comprehensive Psychiatry.* 13:489-492.

## 27. FAMILY GROUP THERAPY

453. Handlon, J.H., and Parloff, M.B. (1962), The Treatment of Patient and Family as a Group: Is It Group Therapy? *International Journal of Group Psychotherapy.* 12:132-141.

454. Glasser, N., and Lewis, J.C. (1965), Evolution of a Treatment Approach to Families: Group Family Therapy. *International Journal of Group Psychotherapy.* 15:505-515.

455. Davies, I.J., et al. (1966), Therapy with a Group of Families in a Psychiatric Day Center. *American Journal of Orthopsychiatry.* 36:134-146.

456. Levin, E.C. (1966), Therapeutic Multiple Family Groups. *International Journal of Group Psychotherapy*. 16:203-208.

457. Harrow, M., et al. (1967), An Investigation into the Nature of the Patient-Family Therapy Group. *American Journal of Orthopsychiatry*. 37:888-899.

458. Coughlin, F., and Wimberger, H.C. (1968), Group Family Therapy. *Family Process*. 7:37-50.

459. Paul, N.L., and Bloom, J.D. (1970), Multiple-Family Therapy: Secrets and Scapegoating in Family Crisis. *International Journal of Group Psychotherapy*. 20:37-47.

460. Leichter, E., and Schulman, G.L. (1972), Interplay of Group and Family Treatment Techniques in Multi-Family Group Therapy. *International Journal of Group Psychotherapy*. 22:167-176.

461. Luber, R.F., and Wells, R.A. (1977), Structured, Short-Term Multiple Family Therapy: An Educational Approach. *International Journal of Group Psychotherapy*. 27:43-58.

462. Strelnick, A.H. (1977), Multiple Family Group Therapy--A Review of Literature. *Family Process*. 16:307-325.

463. Lansky, R., et al. (1978), Multiple Family Groups as Aftercare. *International Journal of Group Psychotherapy*. 28:211-223.

## 28. TIME-LIMITED GROUPS

464. Pine, I.; Gardner, M.; and Lippit, D.L. (1958), Experiences in Short Term Group Psychotherapy. *International Journal of Group Psychotherapy*. 8:275-284.

465. Wolf, A. (1965), Short-term Group Psychotherapy. In: *Short-Term Psychotherapy*, ed. L.R. Wolberg. New York: Grune & Stratton, pp. 219-255.

466. Sadock, B.J., et al. (1968), Short-Term Group Psychotherapy in a Psychiatric Walk-In Clinic. *American Journal of Orthopsychiatry*. 38:724-732.

467. Shrader, W.K., et al. (1969), A Didactic Approach to Structure in Short-Term Group Therapy. *American Journal of Orthopsychiatry*. 39:493-497.

468. Maxmen, J.S. (1973), Group Therapy as Viewed by Hospitalized Patients. *Archives of General Psychiatry*. 28:404-408.

469. Bernard, H.S., and Klein, R.H. (1977), Some Perspectives on Time Limited Group Psychotherapy. *Comprehensive Psychiatry*. 18:579-584.

470. Waxer, P.H. (1977), Short-Term Group Psychotherapy: Some Principles and Techniques. *International Journal of Group Psychotherapy*. 27:33-42.

## 29. CRISIS GROUPS

471. Bloch, H.S. (1968), An Open-ended Crisis-oriented Group for the Poor Who Are Sick. *Archives of General Psychiatry*. 18:178-185.

472. Allgeyer, J.M. (1970), The Crisis Group: Its Unique Usefulness to the Disadvantaged. *International Journal of Group Psychotherapy*. 20:235-240.

473. Trakas, D.A., and Lloyd, G. (1971), Emergency Management in a Short-Term Open Group. *Comprehensive Psychiatry*. 12:170-175.

474. Allgeyer, J. (1973), Using Groups in a Crisis-oriented Outpatient Setting. *International Journal of Group Psychotherapy.* 23:217-222.

475. Donovan, J.; Bennett, M.; and McElroy, C. (1979), The Crisis Group--An Outcome Study. *American Journal of Psychiatry.* 136:906-910.

## 30. AFTER CARE GROUPS

476. Blau, D., and Zilbach, J. (1954), The Use of Group Psychotherapy in Post Hospitalization Treatment: A Clinical Report. *American Journal of Psychiatry.* 111:244-247.

477. Scher, M., and Johnson, M. (1964), Attendance Fluctuations in an After-Care Group. *International Journal of Group Psychotherapy.* 14:223-224.

478. McGee, T.F., and Racusen, F.R. (1967), Alumni Group Therapy as a Form of Aftercare Program. *International Journal of Group Psychotherapy.* 17:243-247.

479. Astrachan, B.M., and Detre, T.P. (1968), Post Hospital Treatment of the Psychotic Patient. *Comprehensive Psychiatry.* 9:71-80.

480. McGee, T., and Racusen, F. (1968), An Evaluation of Alumni Group Psychotherapy: For Patients Discharged from a Group Living Program. *Archives of General Psychiatry.* 18:420-427.

481. Scher, M. (1973), Observations in an Aftercare Group. *International Journal of Group Psychotherapy.* 23:322-337.

482. Grobman, J. (1978), Achieving Cohesiveness in Therapy Groups of Chronically Disturbed Patients. *Group.* 2:141-148.

## 31. GROUP THERAPY IN COMMUNITY PSYCHIATRY

483. Christmas, J.J. (1965), Group Therapy Programs with the Socially Deprived in Community Psychiatry. *International Journal of Group Psychotherapy.* 15:464-476.

484. Beck, J.C., et al. (1968), Learning to Treat the Poor: A Group Experience. *International Journal of Group Psychotherapy.* 18:325-336.

485. Peck, H.B., and Scheidlinger, S. (1968), Group Therapy with the Socially Disadvantaged. In: *Current Psychiatric Therapies*, ed. J.H. Masserman. New York: Grune & Stratton, pp. 173-181.

486. Scheidlinger, S. (1968), Therapeutic Group Approaches in Community Mental Health. *Social Work.* 13:87-95.

487. Beck, J.C. (1969), Outpatient Group Therapy of the Poor. In: *Current Psychiatric Therapies*, ed. J.H. Masserman. New York: Grune & Stratton, pp. 241-244.

488. Pattison, E.M. (1970), Group Psychotherapy and Group Methods in Community Mental Health Programs. *International Journal of Group Psychotherapy.* 20:516-539.

## 32. TEACHING AND LEARNING GROUP PSYCHOTHERAPY

A. Issues in Learning Group Psychotherapy

489. Williams, M. (1966), Limitations, Fantasies and Security Operations of Beginning Group Psychotherapists. *International Journal of Group Psychotherapy.* 16:150-162.

490. Yalom, I.D. (1966), Problems of Neophyte Group Therapists. *Journal of Social Psychiatry*. 12:52-59.

491. Horwitz, L. (1968), Group Psychotherapy Training for Psychiatric Residents. In: *Current Psychiatric Therapies*, ed. J.H. Masserman. New York: Grune & Stratton, pp. 223-232.

492. Almond, R., and Astrachan, B. (1969), Social System Training for Psychiatric Residents. *Psychiatry*. 22:277-291.

493. Berger, I.L. (1969), Resistances to Learning Process in Group Dynamics Programs. *American Journal of Psychiatry*. 126:850-857.

494. Lakin, M.; Lieberman, M.; and Whitaker, D. (1969), Issues in the Training of Group Psychotherapists. *International Journal of Group Psychotherapy*. 19:307-325.

495. Redlich, F.C., and Astrachan, B. (1969), Group Dynamics Training. *American Journal of Psychiatry*. 125:55-61.

496. Chance, E. (1971), Recurrent Problems in the Management of Treatment Groups. *International Journal of Social Psychiatry*. 17:210-216.

497. Horwitz, L. (1971), Training Issues in Group Psychotherapy. *Bulletin of the Menninger Clinic*. 35:249-261.

498. MacLennan, B.W. (1971), Simulated Situations in Group Psychotherapy Training. *International Journal of Group Psychotherapy*. 21:330-332.

499. Anderson, B.N., et al. (1972), Resident Training in Co-therapy Groups. *International Journal of Group Psychotherapy*. 22:192-198.

500. Goldberg, D.A., and Goodman, B. (1973), The Small Group System and Training on an Acute Psychiatric Ward. *Psychiatry in Medicine.* 4:173-182.

501. Pinney, E.L., Jr.; Wells, S.H.; and Fisher, B. (1978), Group Therapy Training in Psychiatric Residency Programs: A National Survey. *American Journal of Psychiatry.* 12:1505-1508.

B. Supervision of Group Psychotherapy

502. Gans, R.W. (1957), The Use of Group Co-Therapist in the Teaching of Psychotherapy. *American Journal of Psychotherapy.* 11:618-625.

503. Geller, J. (1958), Supervision in a Hospital Group Psychotherapy Program. *International Journal of Group Psychotherapy.* 8:313-322.

504. Grotjahn, M. (1960), Supervision of Analytic Group Psychotherapy. *Group Psychotherapy.* 13:161-169.

505. Kanter, S., and Levin, S. (1964), Some General Considerations in the Supervision of Beginning Group Psychotherapists. *International Journal of Group Psychotherapy.* 14:318-331.

506. Podnos, B., and Robinson, L. (1967), A Dynamic Approach to Supervision of Trainees for Group Psychotherapy. *International Journal of Group Psychotherapy.* 17:257-260.

507. McGee, T.F. (1968), Supervision in Group Psychotherapy: A Comparison of Four Approaches. *International Journal of Group Psychotherapy.* 18:165-176.

508. Mintz, E.E. (1968), Group Supervision for Mature Therapists. *Journal of Group Psychoanalysis and Process.* 1:63-70.

509. Glatzer, H.T. (1971), Analytic Supervision in Group Psychotherapy. *International Journal of Group Psychotherapy.* 21:436-443.

510. Lanning, W.L. (1971), A Study of the Relation between Group and Individual Supervision and Three Relationship Measures. *Journal of Counseling Psychology.* 18:401-406.

511. Hare, R.T., and Frankena, S.T. (1972), Peer Group Supervision. *American Journal of Orthopsychiatry.* 42:527-529.

512. Grossman, W.K., and Karmiol, E. (1973), Group Psychotherapy Supervision and Its Effect on Resident Training. *American Journal of Psychiatry.* 130:920-921.

513. McGee, T.F. (1974), The Triadic Approach to Supervision in Group Therapy. *International Journal of Group Psychotherapy.* 24:471-476.

514. Bloch, S., et al. (1975), The Use of a Written Summary in Group Psychotherapy Supervision. *American Journal of Psychiatry.* 132:1055-1057.

515. Mintz, E.E. (1978), Group Supervision: An Experiential Approach. *International Journal of Group Psychotherapy.* 28:467-479.

C. Training Groups

516. Arsenian, J., and Semrad, E.V. (1951), Application of Analytic Observations to Teaching Group Dynamics. *Journal of Psychiatric Social Work.* 20:143-157.

517. Semrad, E.V., and Arsenian, J. (1951), The Use of Group Processes in Teaching Group Dynamics. *American Journal of Psychiatry.* 108:358-363.

518. Kamin, I. (1966), Group Psychotherapy with Residents. In: *Current Psychiatric Therapies*, ed. J.H. Masserman. New York: Grune & Stratton, pp. 157-162.

519. Ammon, G., and Ament, A. (1967), The Terminal Phase of the Dynamic Process of a Group-Dynamic Teaching Group. *International Journal of Group Psychotherapy*. 17:35-43.

520. Day, M. (1967), The Natural History of Training Groups. *International Journal of Group Psychotherapy*. 17:436-446.

521. Horwitz, L. (1967), Training Groups for Psychiatric Residents. *International Journal of Group Psychotherapy*. 17:421-435.

522. Kaplan, S. (1967), Therapy Groups and Training Groups: Similarities and Differences. *International Journal of Group Psychotherapy*. 17:473-504.

523. Jarvis, P.E., and Esty, J.F. (1968), The Alternate-Therapist-Observer Technique in Group Therapy Training. *International Journal of Group Psychotherapy*. 18:95-99.

524. Astrachan, B.M., and Redlich, F.C. (1969), Leadership Ambiguity and Its Effect on Residents' Study Groups. *International Journal of Group Psychotherapy*. 19:487-494.

525. Berger, M.M. (1969), Experiential and Didactic Aspects of Training in Therapeutic Group Approaches. *American Journal of Psychiatry*. 126:845-850.

526. Grotjahn, M. (1969), Analytic Group Therapy with Psychotherapists. *International Journal of Group Psychotherapy*. 19:326-333.

527. Sadock, B.J., and Kaplan, H.I. (1969), Group Psychotherapy with Psychiatric Residents. *International Journal of Group Psychotherapy*. 19:475-486.

528. Sadock, B.J., and Kaplan, H.I. (1970), Long-Term Intensive Group Psychotherapy with Psychiatric Residents as Part of Residency Training. *American Journal of Psychiatry*. 126:1138-1143.

529. Sherman, R.W., and Hildreth, A.M. (1970), A Resident Group Process Training Seminar. *American Journal of Psychiatry*. 127:372-375.

530. Volkan, V.D., and Hawkins, D.R. (1972), The Learning Group. *American Journal of Psychiatry*. 128:1121-1125.

531. Spotnitz, H. (1975), Experiences in Conducting Demonstration Groups. In: *Group Therapy 1975: An Overview*, ed. M.L. Aronson and L.R. Wolberg. New York: Stratton Intercontinental Medical Book Corp., pp. 219-231.


## 33. GROUP RELATIONS

532. Musto, D.F., and Astrachan, B.M. (1968), Strange Encounter: The Use of Study Groups with Graduate Students in History. *Psychiatry*. 31:264-276.

533. Papanek, H. (1969), Therapeutic and Antitherapeutic Factors in Group Relations. *American Journal of Psychotherapy*. 23:396-404.

534. Rioch, M.J. (1970), Group Relations: Rationale and Technique. *International Journal of Group Psychotherapy*. 20:340-355.

535. Menninger, R.W. (1972), The Impact of Group Relations Conferences on Organizational Growth. *International Journal of Group Psychotherapy*. 22:415-432.

536. Rioch, M.J. (1977), The A.K. Rice Group Relations Conferences as a Reflection of Society. *Journal of Personality and Social Systems*. 1:1-16.

## 34. GROUP THERAPY IN A MEDICAL SETTING (INCLUDING PSYCHOSOMATIC PATIENTS)

537. Deutsch, A.L., and Lippman, A. (1964), Group Psychotherapy for Patients with Psychosomatic Illness. *Psychosomatics*. 5:14-20.

538. Slawson, P.F. (1965), Group Psychotherapy with Obese Woman. *Psychosomatics*. 6:206-209.

539. Berger, M.M., and Rosenbaum, M. (1967), Notes on Help-Rejecting Complainers. *International Journal of Group Psychotherapy*. 17:357-370.

540. Adsett, C.A., et al. (1968), Short-Term Group Psychotherapy for Post-Myocardial Infarction Patients and Their Wives. *Canadian Medical Association Journal*. 99:577-584.

541. Kornhaber, A. (1968), Group Treatment of Obesity. *GP*. 38:116-120.

542. Shambaugh, P.W., and Kanter, S.S. (1969), Spouses Under Stress: Group Meetings with Spouses of Patients on Hemodialysis. *American Journal of Psychiatry*. 125:928-936.

543. Mone, L.C. (1970), Short-Term Group Psychotherapy with Postcardiac Patients. *International Journal of Group Psychotherapy*. 20:99-108.

544. Bilodeau, C.B., and Hackett, T.P. (1971), Issues Raised in a Group Setting by Patients Recovering from Myocardial Infarction. *American Journal of Psychiatry*. 128:105-110.

545. Pattison, E., et al. (1971), Response to Group Treatment in Patients with Severe Chronic Lung Disease. *International Journal of Group Psychotherapy*. 21:214-225.

546. Reckless, J.B. (1971), A Behavioral Treatment of Bronchial Asthma in Modified Group Therapy. *Psychosomatics*. 12:168-173.

547. Hollon, T.H. (1972), Modified Group Therapy in the Treatment of Patients on Chronic Hemodialysis. *American Journal of Psychotherapy*. 26:501-510.

548. Lassiter, R.E., and Willett, A.B. (1973), Interaction of Group Co-therapists in the Multidisciplinary Team Treatment of Obesity. *International Journal of Group Psychotherapy*. 23:82-92.

549. Mann, W., et al. (1973), The Use of Group Counseling Procedures in the Rehabilitation of Spinal Cord Injured Patients. *American Journal of Occupational Therapy*. 27:73-77.

550. Murphy, A., et al. (1973), Group Work with Parents of Children with Down's Syndrome. *Social Casework*. 54:114-119.

551. Ohlmeier, D., et al. (1973), Psychoanalytic Group Interviews and Short-Term Group Psychotherapy with Post-Myocardial Infarction Patients. *Psychiatric Clinica*. 6:240-249.

552. Rahe, H., et al. (1973), Group Therapy in the Outpatient Management of Post-Myocardial Infarction Patients. *Psychiatry in Medicine*. 4:77-88.

553. Cladwell, H.S.; Leveque, K.I.; and Lane, D.M. (1974), Group Psychotherapy in the Management of Hemophilia. *Psychological Reports*. 35:339-342.

554. Ammon, G. (1975), Analytic Group Psychotherapy as an Instrument for the Treatment and Research of Psychosomatic Disorders. In: *Group Therapy 1975: An Overview*, ed. M.L. Aronson and L.R. Wolberg. New York: Stratton Intercontinental Medical Book Corp., pp. 127-144.

555. Bayrakal, S. (1975), A Group Experience with Chronically Disabled Adolescents. *American Journal of Psychiatry*. 132:1291-1294.

556. Oradei, D.M., and Waite, N.S. (1975), Group Psychotherapy with Stroke Patients During the Immediate Recovery Phase. *Nursing Digest*. 3:26-29.

557. Singler, J.R. (1975), Group Work with Hospitalized Stroke Patients. *Social Casework*. 56:348-353.

558. Fisher, B., and Laufer, L. (1977), A Survey of the Literature on Psychological Factors in Heart Attack Patients to Group Psychotherapy, and Recommendations for Further Investigation. In: *Group Therapy 1977: An Overview*, ed. L.R. Wolberg. New York: Stratton Intercontinental Medical Book Corp., pp. 219-222.

559. Ford, C.V., and Long, K.D. (1977), Group Psychotherapy of Somatizing Patients. *Psychotherapy and Psychosomatics*. 28:294-304.

560. Roberts, J.P. (1977), The Problems of Group Psychotherapy for Psychosomatic Patients. *Psychotherapy and Psychosomatics*. 28:305-315.

561. Gilder, R., et al. (1978), Group Therapy with Parents of Children with Leukemia. *American Journal of Psychotherapy*. 32:276-287.

562. Udelman, H., and Udelman, D. (1978), Group Therapy with Rheumatoid Arthritic Patients. *American Journal of Psychotherapy*. 32:288-299.

563. Yano, B.; Shabert, J.; and Alexander, L. (1979), A Psychiatrist-Nutritionist Group Therapy Approach to the Treatment of Obesity. *International Journal of Group Psychotherapy.* 29:185-194.

## 35. GROUPS WITH DOCTORS AND MEDICAL STUDENTS

564. Balint, M.; Ball, D.; and Hare, M. (1969), Training Medical Students in Patient-Centered Medicine. *Comprehensive Psychiatry.* 10:249-258.

565. Bacal, H. (1972), Balint Groups: Training or Treatment? *Psychiatry in Medicine.* 3:373-377.

566. Chertok, L., and Bourguignon, O. (1972), The Balint Group and Preventive Industrial Medicine. *Psychiatry in Medicine.* 3:395-402.

567. Knoepfel, H. (1972), The Effects of the Balint Group on Its Members and Leader. *Psychiatry in Medicine.* 3:379-383.

568. Main, T. (1972), Michael Balint and His Contributions. *Psychiatry in Medicine.* 3:403-406.

569. Moreau, A. (1972), Transcript of a Balint Group Session. *Psychiatry in Medicine.* 3:389-394.

570. Morse, S. (1972), The Psychological Theory of Michael Balint. *Psychiatry in Medicine.* 3:407-416.

571. Tredgold, R. (1972), Michael Balint and Medical Students. *Psychiatry in Medicine.* 3:385-388.

572. Selvini, A. (1973), An Internist's Experience in a Doctor-Patient Relationship Training Group (Balint Group). *Psychotherapy & Psychosomatics.* 22:1-18.

## 36. WOMEN'S GROUPS

573. Fried, E. (1974), Does Woman's New Self-Concept Call for New Approaches in Group Psychotherapy? *International Journal of Group Psychotherapy.* 24:265-272.

574. Bernardez-Bonesatti, T. (1978), Women's Groups: A Feminist Perspective on the Treatment of Women. In: *Changing Approaches to the Psychotherapies*, ed. H. Grayson and C. Loew. New York: Spectrum Publications, pp. 55-67.

## 37. ASSERTIVENESS TRAINING GROUPS

575. Field, G.D. (1975), Group Assertive Training, Training for Severely Disturbed Patients. *Journal of Behavior Therapy in Experimental Psychiatry.* 6:129-134.

576. Rose, S., and Schinke, S. (1978), Assertive Training. In: *Changing Approaches to the Psychotherapies*, ed. H. Grayson and C. Loew. New York: Spectrum Publications, pp. 3-33.

## 38. GROUPS FOR HOLOCAUST SURVIVORS

577. Fogelman, M.A., and Savran, B. (1979), Therapeutic Groups for Children of Holocaust Survivors. *International Journal of Group Psychotherapy.* 29:211-235.

## 39. IN-PATIENT GROUPS

578. Pine, I.; Gardner, M.; and Lippit, D.L. (1958), Experiences in Short Term Group Psychotherapy. *International Journal of Group Psychotherapy.* 8:275-284.

579. Beran, M. (1961), Combined Individual and Group Therapy within a Hospital Team Set-Up. *International Journal of Group Psychotherapy.* 11:313-318.

580. Astrachan, B.M., et al. (1967), The Unled Patient Group as a Therapeutic Tool. *International Journal of Group Psychotherapy.* 17:178-191.

581. Pattison, E.M., et al. (1967), Assessing Specific Effects of Inpatient Group Psychotherapy. *International Journal of Group Psychotherapy.* 17:283-297.

582. Slavson, S.R. (1969), Vita-erg Therapy with Long-term Regressed Psychotic Women. In: *Social Psychiatry*, ed. N. Petrilowitsch and H. Flegel. New York and Basel: S. Karger, pp. 104-120.

583. Moadel, Y. (1970), Adolescent Group Psychotherapy in a Hospital Setting. *American Journal of Psychoanalysis.* 30:68-72.

584. Chertoff, H.R., et al. (1971), A Technique for Overcoming Resistance to Group Therapy in Psychotic Patients on a Community Mental Health Service. *International Journal of Group Psychotherapy.* 21:53-61.

585. Richmond, A.H., and Slagle, S. (1971), Some Notes on the Inhibition of Aggression in an Inpatient Psychotherapy Group. *International Journal of Group Psychotherapy.* 21:333-338.

586. Elmore, J.L., and Saunders, R. (1972), Group Encounter Techniques in the Short-Term Psychiatric Hospital. *American Journal of Psychotherapy.* 26:490-500.

587. Maxmen, J.S. (1973), Group Therapy as Viewed by Hospitalized Patients. *Archives of General Psychiatry.* 28:404-408.

588. Leopold, H.S. (1976), Selective Group Approaches with Psychotic Patients in Hospital Settings. *American Journal of Psychotherapy.* 30:95-103.

589. Fleischl, M. (1977), Group Approaches in a Day Hospital Setting. In: *Group Therapy 1977: An Overview*, ed. L.R. Wolberg. New York: Stratton Intercontinental Medical Book Corp., pp. 233-238.

590. Arriaga, K., et al. (1978), Group Therapy Evaluation for Psychiatric Inpatients. *International Journal of Group Psychotherapy.* 28:359-364.

591. Bailis, S.S.; Lambert, S.R.; and Bernstein, S.B. (1978), The Legacy of the Group: A Study of Group Therapy with a Transient Membership. *Social Work in Health Care.* 3:405-418.

592. Cory, T.L., and Page, D. (1978), Group Techniques for Effecting Change in the More Disturbed Patient. *Group.* 2:149-155.

593. Druck, A.B. (1978), The Role of Didactic Group Psychotherapy in Short-Term Psychiatric Settings. *Group.* 2:98-109.

594. Kibel, H.D. (1978), The Rationale for the Use of Group Psychotherapy for Borderline Patients on a Short-Term Unit. *International Journal of Group Psychotherapy.* 28:339-358.

595. Maxmen, J.S. (1978), An Educative Model for Inpatient Group Therapy. *International Journal of Group Psychotherapy.* 28:321-338.

## 40. LARGE GROUPS

596. Mitscherlich, A. (1971), Psychoanalysis and the Aggression of Large Groups. *International Journal of Psychoanalysis*. 52:161-167.

597. de Mare, P. (1975), The Politics of Large Groups. In: *The Large Group: Dynamics and Therapy*, ed. L. Kreeger. Itasca, Ill.: Peacock Publishers, pp. 145-158.

598. Foulkes, S.H. (1975), Problems of the Large Group from a Group-Analytic Point of View. In: *The Large Group: Dynamics and Therapy*, ed. L. Kreeger. Itasca, Ill.: Peacock Publishers, pp. 33-56.

599. Hooper, M. (1975), Large Groups in Natural Settings-- An Anthropological View. In: *The Large Group: Dynamics and Therapy*, ed. L. Kreeger. Itasca, Ill.: Peacock Publishers, pp. 252-271.

600. Hopper, E., and Weyman, A. (1975), A Sociological View of Large Groups. In: *The Large Group: Dynamics and Therapy*, ed. L. Kreeger. Itasca, Ill.: Peacock Publishers, pp. 159-192.

601. Main, T. (1975), Some Psychodynamics of Large Groups. In: *The Large Group: Dynamics and Therapy*, ed. L. Kreeger. Itasca, Ill.: Peacock Publishers, pp. 57-86.

602. Skynner, A.C.R. (1975), The Large Group in Training. In: *The Large Group: Dynamics and Therapy*, ed. L. Kreeger. Itasca, Ill.: Peacock Publishers, pp. 227-251.

603. Springmann, R. (1975), Psychotherapy in the Large Group. In: *The Large Group: Dynamics and Therapy*, ed. L. Kreeger. Itasca, Ill.: Peacock Publishers, pp. 212-226.

604. Turquet, P. (1975), Threats to Identity in the Large Group. In: *The Large Group: Dynamics and Therapy*, ed. L. Kreeger. Itasca, Ill.: Peacock Publishers, pp. 87-144.

605. Whiteley, J.S. (1975), The Large Group as a Medium for Sociotherapy. In: *The Large Group: Dynamics and Therapy*, ed. L. Kreeger. Itasca, Ill.: Peacock Publishers, pp. 193-211.

## 41. ACTIVITIES IN GROUP THERAPY

606. Kramish, A. (1965), Letter Reading in Group Psychotherapy. *Group Psychotherapy*. 9:40-43.

607. Butler, B. (1966), Music Group Psychotherapy. *Journal of Music Therapy*. 3:53-56.

608. Daniels, D.N. (1969), Task Groups in the Therapy of Mental Patients. In: *Current Psychiatric Therapies*, ed. J.H. Masserman. New York: Grune & Stratton, pp. 186-194.

609. Fidler, G.S. (1969), The Task-Oriented Group as a Context for Treatment. *American Journal of Occupational Therapy*. 23:43-48.

610. Riess, B.F. (1969), Developments in Dance Therapy. In: *Current Psychiatric Therapies*, ed. J.H. Masserman. New York: Grune & Stratton, pp. 195-201.

611. Bell, R.W. (1970), Activity as a Tool in Group Therapy. *Perspectives in Psychiatric Care*. 8:84-91.

612. Dickens, G., and Sharpe, M. (1970), Music Therapy in the Setting of a Psychotherapeutic Center. *British Journal of Medical Psychology*. 43:83-94.

613. Denny, J.M. (1972), Techniques for Individual and Group Art Therapy. *American Journal of Art Therapy*. 11:117-134.

614. Buck, L.A., and Kramer, A. (1974), Poetry as a Means of Group Facilitation. *Journal of Humanistic Psychology*. 14:57-71.

615. Kymissis, P. (1977), The Use of Paintings in Analytic Group Psychotherapy. In: *Group Therapy 1977: An Overview*, ed. L.R. Wolberg. New York: Stratton Intercontinental Medical Book Corp., pp. 129-136.

616. Garai, J. (1978), Art Therapy--Catalyst for Creative Expression and Personality Integration. In: *Changing Approaches to the Psychotherapies*, ed. H. Grayson and C. Lowe. New York: Spectrum Publications, pp. 69-116.


## 42. THERAPEUTIC MILIEU AND THE GROUP PROCESS

A. General Issues and Definitions

617. Fromm-Reichmann, F. (1947), Problems of Therapeutic Management in a Psychoanalytic Hospital. *Psychoanalytic Quarterly*. 16:325-356.

618. Caudill, W., et al. (1952), Social Structure and Interaction Process on a Psychiatric Ward. *American Journal of Orthopsychiatry*. 22:314-334.

619. Rioch, D.M., and Stanton, A.H. (1953), Milieu in Psychiatric Treatment. *Proceedings of the Associates for Research in Nervous and Mental Diseases*. Baltimore: Williams & Wilkins, 21:94-105.

620. Schwartz, M. (1957), What is a Therapeutic Milieu? In: *The Patient and the Mental Hospital*, ed.

M. Greenblatt, Levinson, and Williams. Glencoe, Ill.: The Free Press, pp. 130-144.

621. Cumming, E., and Cumming, J. (1962), *Ego and Milieu: Theory and Practice of Environmental Therapy.* Chicago: Aldine-Atherton.

622. Morrice, J.K.W. (1964), The Ward as a Therapeutic Group. *British Journal of Medical Psychology.* 37:157-165.

623. Berne, E. (1968), Staff-patient Conferences. *American Journal of Psychiatry.* 125:286-293.

624. Abroms, G.M. (1969), Defining Milieu Therapy. *Archives of General Psychiatry.* 21:553-560.

625. Almond, R., et al. (1969), Milieu Therapeutic Process. *Archives of General Psychiatry.* 21:431-442.

626. Astrachan, B.M., et al. (1970), Systems Approach to Day Hospitalization. *Archives of General Psychiatry.* 22:550-559.

627. Marohn, R.C. (1970), The Therapeutic Milieu as an Open System. *Archives of General Psychiatry.* 22:360-364.

628. Ellsworth, R., et al. (1971), Milieu Characteristics of Successful Psychiatric Treatment Programs. *American Journal of Orthopsychiatry.* 41:427-441.

629. Lewis, D.J. (1971), Some Approaches to the Evaluation of Milieu Therapy. *Canadian Psychiatric Association Journal.* 16:203-208.

630. Stauble, W.J. (1971), Milieu Therapy and the Therapeutic Community. *Canadian Psychiatric Association Journal.* 16:197-202.

631. White, N.L. (1972), The Descent of Milieu Therapy. *Canadian Psychiatric Association Journal.* 17:41-50.

632. Stannard, D.L. (1973), Ideological Conflict on a Psychiatric Ward. *Psychiatry*. 36:143-156.

633. Almond, R. (1975), Issues in Milieu Treatment. *Schizophrenia Bulletin*. 13:12-36.

634. Almond, R. (1975), *The Healing Community: Dynamics of the Therapeutic Milieu*. New York: Aronson.

635. Fidler, J.W. (1975), The Day Hospital: A Multimodal Group. In: *Group Therapy 1975: An Overview*, ed. M.L. Aronson and L.R. Wolberg. New York: Stratton Intercontinental Medical Book Corp., pp. 38-48.

B. Therapeutic Milieu vs. Therapeutic Community

636. Stanton, A., and Schwartz, M. (1954), Pathologic Excitement and Hidden Staff Disagreement; Incontinence; and Morale and Its Breakdown. In: *The Mental Hospital*. New York: Basic Books.

637. Jones, M. (1957), The Treatment of Personality Disorders in a Therapeutic Community. *Psychiatry*. 20:211-220.

638. Jones, M., and Rappaport, R. (1957), The Absorption of New Doctors into a Therapeutic Community. In: *The Patient and the Mental Hospital*, ed. M. Greenblatt, Levinson, and Williams. Glencoe, Ill.: The Free Press, pp. 248-262.

639. Rashkis, H.A., and Wallace, A.F.C. (1959), The Reciprocal Effect: How Patient Disturbance Affects and Is Affected by Staff Attitudes. *Archives of General Psychiatry*. 9:489-498.

640. Stubblebine, J.M. (1960), The Therapeutic Community: A Further Formulation. *Mental Hospitals*. 11:16-18.

641. Jones, M. (1964), A Passing Glance at the Therapeutic Community in 1964. *International Journal of Group Psychotherapy.* 14:5-10.

642. Jones, M. (1968), *Beyond the Therapeutic Community.* New Haven: Yale University Press.

643. Raskin, D.E. (1971), Problems in the Therapeutic Community. *American Journal of Psychiatry.* 128:492.

644. Rosenhan, D.L. (1973), On Being Sane in Insane Places. *Science.* 179:250-258.

C. Group Therapy in the Therapeutic Milieu

*i. General Issues*

645. Rostov, B.W. (1965), Group Work in the Psychiatric Hospital: A Critical Review of the Literature. *Social Work.* 10:23-31.

646. Jones, M. (1966), Group Work in Mental Hospitals. *British Journal of Psychiatry.* 112:1007-1011.

647. Durkin, H. (1967), Levels of Group Therapy in Large Hospitals. *American Journal of Orthopsychiatry.* 37:272.

648. Stein, A. (1971), Group Interaction and Group Psychotherapy in a General Hospital. *Mt. Sinai Journal of Medicine.* 38:89-100.

649. Bugh, V.G. (1972), Group Psychotherapy in the Mental Hospital. *Comparative Group Studies.* 3:99-103.

650. Battegay, R. (1974), Group Psychotherapy as a Method of Treatment in a Psychiatric Hospital. In: *The Challenge for Group Psychotherapy Present and Future*, ed. S. deSchill. New York: International Universities Press, pp. 173-230.

651. Frank, J. (1975), Group Therapy in the Mental Hospital. In: *Group Psychotherapy and Group Function*, ed. M. Rosenbaum and M.M. Berger. New York: Basic Books, pp. 465-482.

*ii. Large Milieu Groups*

652. Jones, M., and Hollingsworth, S. (1963), Work with Large Groups in Mental Hospitals. *Journal of Individual Psychology*. 19:61-68.

653. Mack, J. (1963), The Evolution of Patient Ward Meetings into Group Psychotherapy. *International Journal of Social Psychiatry*. 9:51-57.

654. Kernberg, P.F. (1965), Experiences with Open Groups on a State Hospital Admission Ward. *Bulletin of the Menninger Clinic*. 29:27-34.

655. Horowitz, M.J., and Weisberg, P. (1966), Techniques for the Group Psychotherapy of Acute Psychosis. *International Journal of Group Psychotherapy*. 16:42-50.

656. Prosen, H., and Lamberd, W.G. (1966), Movement in a Ward Community Group as a Reflection of Patient Change. *International Journal of Group Psychotherapy*. 16:291-303.

657. Curry, A.E. (1967), Large Therapeutic Groups: A Critique and Appraisal of Selected Literature. *International Journal of Group Psychotherapy*. 17:536-547.

658. Marohn, R.C. (1967), The Unit Meeting: Its Implications for a Therapeutic Correctional Community. *International Journal of Group Psychotherapy*. 17:159-167.

659. Matkon, A. (1967), Community Meetings on the Admission Ward. *Hospital and Community Psychiatry*. 18:206-209.

660. Schiff, S.B., and Glassman, S.M. (1969), Large and Small Group Therapy in a State Mental Health Center. *International Journal of Group Psychotherapy.* 19:150-157.

661. Hershelman, P., and Freundlich, D. (1970), Group Therapy with Multiple Therapists in a Large Group. *American Journal of Psychiatry.* 127:457-461.

662. Springmann, R.R. (1970), A Large Group. *International Journal of Group Psychotherapy.* 20:210-218.

663. Buck, R.E. (1972), A Large Milieu Therapy Group. *American Journal of Psychotherapy.* 26:384-393.

664. Foulkes, S.H. (1975), Problems of the Large Group from a Group Analytic Point of View. In: *The Large Group: Dynamics and Therapy,* ed. L. Kreeger, Itasca, Ill.: Peacock Publishers, pp. 33-56.

665. Main, T. (1975), Some Psychodynamics of Large Groups. In: *The Large Group: Dynamics and Therapy,* ed. L. Kreeger. Itasca, Ill.: Peacock Publishers, pp. 57-86.

666. Skynner, R. (1975), The Large Group in Training. In: *The Large Group: Dynamics and Therapy,* ed. L. Kreeger. Itasca, Ill.: Peacock Publishers, pp. 227-251.

667. Turquet, P. (1975), Threats to Identity in the Large Group. In: *The Large Group: Dynamics and Therapy,* ed. L. Kreeger. Itasca, Ill.: Peacock Publishers, pp. 87-144.

*iii. Small Milieu Groups*

668. Laffel, J., and Sarason, I. (1957), Limited Goal Group Psychotherapy on a Locked Service. *Diseases of the Nervous System.* 18:63-66.

669. Klapman, J.W. (1959), The Unselected Group in Mental Hospitals and Group Treatment of Chronic Schizophrenics. *Diseases of the Nervous System.* 20:17-23.

670. Winick, C., and Holt, H. (1960), Uses of Music in Group Psychotherapy. *Group Psychotherapy and Psychodrama.* 13:76-86.

671. Niver, E.O., et al. (1965), Exercise as Group Therapy. *Mental Hospitals.* 16:112-113.

672. Mack, J.E., and Branum, M.C. (1966), Group Activity and Group Discussion in the Treatment of Hospitalized Psychiatric Patients. *International Journal of Group Psychotherapy.* 16:452-462.

673. Towey, M.R., et al. (1966), Group Activities with Psychiatric In-Patients. *Social Work.* 11:50-56.

674. Lazarus, H.R., and Bienlein, D.K. (1967), Soap Opera Therapy. *International Journal of Group Psychotherapy.* 17:252-256.

675. Bartz, W.R. (1970), A Small-Group Approach on State Hospital Wards. *Hospital and Community Psychiatry.* 21:390-393.

676. Slivkin, S.E. (1970), One-to-One Psychotherapy in a Group Setting with Hospitalized Psychotic Patients. *International Journal of Group Psychotherapy.* 20:63-76.

677. Steffens, E. (1970), Using Literature in Group Therapy. *Hospital and Community Psychiatry.* 21:227.

678. Lehrer-Carle, I. (1971), Group Music with Schizophrenics. *Journal of Contemporary Psychotherapy.* 2:111-116.

679. Sedlmair, M., and Sisley, E. (1972), Mural Group: Integration of Projective Drawings with Standard Verbal Group Therapy Techniques. *Psychological Reports.* 31:475-481.

680. Steiner, J. (1973), The Use of Activity as an Adjunct to Group Psychotherapy: I. *Groups.* 5:15-28.

681. Wolff, R.A. (1975), Therapeutic Experiences Through Group Art Expression. *American Journal of Art Therapy.* 14:91-98.

## 43. RESEARCH AND OUTCOME STUDIES

682. Kelman, H.C., and Parloff, M.B. (1957), Interrelations Among Three Criteria of Improvement in Group Therapy: Comfort, Effectiveness, and Self-Awareness. *Journal of Abnormal and Social Psychology.* 54:281-288.

683. Yalom, I.D., et al. (1967), Prediction of Improvement in Group Therapy. An Exploratory Study. *Archives of General Psychiatry.* 17:159-168.

684. Parloff, M.B. (1970), Assessing the Effects of Headshrinking and Mind-Expanding. *International Journal of Group Psychotherapy.* 20:14-24.

685. Cabral, R., et al. (1975), Patients' and Observers' Assessments of Process and Outcome in Group Therapy: A Follow-Up Study. *American Journal of Psychiatry.* 132:1052-1054.

686. Dick, B.M. (1975), A Ten Year Study of Out-Patient Analytic Group Therapy. *British Journal of Psychiatry.* 127:365-375.

687. Grunebaum, H. (1975), A Soft-Hearted Review of Hard-Nosed Research on Groups. *International Journal of Group Psychotherapy.* 25:185-197.

688. Malan, D.H., et al. (1976), Group Psychotherapy: A Long-Term Follow-Up Study. *Archives of General Psychiatry.* 33:1303-1315.

689. Parloff, M., and Dies, R. (1977), Group Psychotherapy Outcome Research. *International Journal of Group Psychotherapy*. 27:281-319.

690. Piper, W.E., et al. (1977), An Outcome Study of Group Therapy. *Archives of General Psychiatry*. 34:1027-1032.

## 44. GROUP PSYCHOTHERAPY WITH CHILDREN

### A. General Issues and Overview

691. Redl, F. (1966), What About Groups; Psychoanalysis and Group Therapy: A Developmental Point of View. In: *When We Deal With Children*, ed. F. Redl. New York: The Free Press, pp. 153-235; 309-327.

692. Frank, M.G., and Zilbach, J. (1968), Current Trends in Group Therapy with Children. *International Journal of Group Psychotherapy*. 18:447-460.

693. Kraft, I.A. (1968), An Overview of Group Therapy with Adolescents. *International Journal of Group Psychotherapy*. 18:461-468.

694. Johnson, D.L., and Gold, S.R. (1971), An Empirical Approach to Issues of Selection and Evaluation in Group Therapy. *International Journal of Group Psychotherapy*. 21:456-469.

695. Barcai, A., et al. (1973), A Comparison of Three Group Approaches to Under-Achieving Children. *American Journal of Orthopsychiatry*. 43:133-141.

B. Young Children

696. Haizlip, T., et al. (1975), Issues in Developing Psychotherapy Groups for Preschool Children in Outpatient Clinics. *American Journal of Psychiatry.* 132:1061-1063.

C. Psychotic Children

697. King, C.H. (1959), Activity Group Therapy with a Schizophrenic Boy: Follow-Up Two Years Later. *International Journal of Group Psychotherapy.* 9:184-194.

698. Goldfarb, W., and Radin, S.S. (1964), Group Behavior of Schizophrenic Children. *International Journal of Social Psychiatry.* 10:199-208.

699. Lieberman, F., and Taylor, S.S. (1965), Combined Group and Individual Treatment of a Schizophrenic Child. *Social Casework.* 46:80-86.

700. Lifton, N., and Smolen, E.M. (1966), Group Psychotherapy with Schizophrenic Children. *International Journal of Group Psychotherapy.* 16:59-69.

701. Gratton, L., and Rizzo, A.E. (1969), Group Therapy with Young Psychotic Children. *International Journal of Group Psychotherapy.* 19:63-71.

D. Activity Group Therapy

702. Ginott, H.G. (1958), Play Group Psychotherapy: A Theoretical Framework. *International Journal of Group Psychotherapy.* 8:410-418.

703. Scheidlinger, S., et al. (1959), Activity Group Therapy in a Family Service Agency. *Social Casework.* 40:193-201.

704. Peck, M., and Stewart, R. (1964), Current Practices in Selection Criteria for a Group Play Therapy. *Journal of Clinical Psychology.* 20:146.

705. Zilbach, J.J., and Grunebaum, M.G. (1964), Pregenital Components in Incest as Manifested in Two Girls in Activity Group Therapy. *International Journal of Group Psychotherapy.* 14:166-177.

706. Egan, M.H. (1975), Dynamisms in Activity Discussion Group Therapy (ADGT). *International Journal of Group Psychotherapy.* 25:199-218.

707. MacLennan, B.W. (1977), Modifications of Activity Group Therapy for Children. *International Journal of Group Psychotherapy.* 27:85-96.

708. Shiffer, M. (1977), Activity-Interview Group Psychotherapy: Theory, Principles, and Practice. *International Journal of Group Psychotherapy.* 27:377-388.


E. Concurrent Group Treatment of Parents and Children

709. LeVay, M., and Rathod, N.H. (1963), Concurrent Treatment Groups of Mothers and Children. *American Journal of Psychiatry.* 119:1169-1171.

710. Jones, H.B. (1969), Group Therapy for Mothers and Children in Parallel. *American Journal of Psychiatry.* 125:1439-1442.


F. Latency Age Children

711. Scheidlinger, S. (1960), Experiential Group Treatment of Severely Deprived Latency-Age Children. *American Journal of Orthopsychiatry.* 30:356-368.

712. Daniels, C.R. (1964), Play Group Therapy with Children. *ACTA Psychotherapeutica*. 12:45-52.

713. Karson, S. (1965), Group Psychotherapy with Latency Age Boys. *International Journal of Group Psychotherapy*. 15:81-89.

714. Scheidlinger, S. (1965), Three Group Approaches with Socially Deprived Latency-Age Children. *International Journal of Group Psychotherapy*. 15:434-445.

715. Leal, M.R.M. (1966), Group-Analytic Play Therapy with Pre-Adolescent Girls. *International Journal of Group Psychotherapy*. 16:58-64.

716. Scheidlinger, S. (1966), The Concept of Latency: Implications for Group Treatment. *Social Casework*. 47:363-367.

717. Barcai, A., and Robinson, E.H. (1969), Conventional Group Therapy with Pre-adolescent Children. *International Journal of Group Psychotherapy*. 19:334-345.

718. Von Scoy, H. (1971), An Activity Group Approach to Seriously Disturbed Latency Boys. *Child Welfare*. 50:413-419.

719. Epstein, N., and Altman, S. (1972), Experiences in Converting an Activity Group into Verbal Group Therapy with Latency-Age Boys. *International Journal of Group Psychotherapy*. 22:93-100.

720. Pelosi, A.A., and Friedman, H. (1974), The Activity Period in Group Psychotherapy. *Psychiatric Quarterly*. 48:223-229.

721. Strunk, C., and Witkin, L.J. (1974), The Transformation of a Latency Age Girls' Group from Unstructured Play to Problem-Focused Discussion. *International Journal of Group Psychotherapy*. 24:460-470.

722. Dannefer, E., et al. (1975), Experience in Developing a Combined Activity and Verbal Group Therapy Program with Latency-Age Boys. *International Journal of Group Psychotherapy*. 25:331-337.

723. Schamess, G. (1976), Group Treatment Modalities for Latency-Age Children. *International Journal of Group Psychotherapy*. 26:455-473.

724. Abramson, R.M.; Hoffman, L.; and Johns, C.A. (1979), Play Group Psychotherapy for Early Latency-Age Children on an Inpatient Psychiatric Unit. *International Journal of Group Psychotherapy*. 29:383-392.

725. Rosenberg, J., and Cherbuliez, T. (1979), Inpatient Group Therapy for Older Children and Pre-Adolescents. *International Journal of Group Psychotherapy*. 29:393-405.

G. Combined Individual and Group Treatment

726. Coolidge, J., and Grunebaum, M. (1964), Individual and Group Therapy of a Latency-Age Child. *International Journal of Group Psychotherapy*. 14:84-96.

H. Adolescents

727. Kassoff, A. (1958), Advantages of Multiple Therapists in a Group of Severely Acting Out Adolescent Boys. *International Journal of Group Psychotherapy*. 8:70-75.

728. Godenne, G.D. (1964), Outpatient Adolescent Group Psychotherapy: I. A Review of the Literature on the Use of Co-Therapists, Psychodrama, and Parent Group Therapy. *American Journal of Psychotherapy*. 18:584-593.

729. Sadock, B. (1964), A Preliminary Report on Short-term Group Psychotherapy on an Acute Adolescent Male Service. *International Journal of Group Psychotherapy.* 14:465-473.

730. James, S.L., et al. (1967), Treatment for Delinquent Girls: The Adolescent Self-Concept Group. *Community Mental Health Journal.* 3:377-381.

731. Jacobs, M.A., and Christ, J. (1967), Structuring and Limit Setting as Techniques in the Group Treatment of Adolescent Delinquents. *Community Mental Health Journal.* 3:237-244.

732. Kraft, I.A. (1968), An Overview of Group Therapy with Adolescents. *International Journal of Group Psychotherapy.* 18:461-468.

733. Dyck, G. (1969), "Talking the Dozens." A Game of Insults Played in a Group of Adolescent Boys. *Bulletin of the Menninger Clinic.* 33:108-117.

734. Rachman, A.W. (1971), Encounter Techniques in Analytic Group Psychotherapy with Adolescents. *International Journal of Group Psychotherapy.* 21:319-329.

735. Greene, R.J., and Crowder, D.L. (1972), Group Therapy with Adolescents: An Integrative Approach. *Journal of Contemporary Psychotherapy.* 5:55-61.

736. Gottsegen, M.G., and Grasso, M. (1973), Group Treatment of the Mother-Daughter Relationship. *International Journal of Group Psychotherapy.* 23:69-81.

737. Kraft, I.A., and Vick, J.W. (1973), Flexibility and Variability of Group Psychotherapy with Adolescent Girls. In: *Group Therapy 1973: An Overview,* ed. L.R. Wolberg and E.K. Schwartz. New York: Intercontinental Medical Book Corp., pp. 71-91.

738. Snow, D.L., and Held, M.L. (1973), Group Psychotherapy with Obese Adolescent Females. *Adolescence.* 8:407-414.

739. Berkovitz, I., and Sugar, M. (1975), Indications and Contra-indications for Adolescent Group Psychotherapy. In: *The Adolescent in Group and Family Therapy*, ed. M. Sugar. New York: Brunner/Mazel, pp. 3-26.

740. Rizzo, A.; Ossoria, A.; and Saxon, L. (1975), The Organization of an Adolescent Unit in a State Hospital: Problems and Attempted Solutions. In: *The Adolescent in Group and Family Therapy*, ed. M. Sugar. New York: Brunner/Mazel, pp. 68-86.

741. Shapiro, R., et al. (1975), The Impact of Group Experiences on Adolescent Development. In: *The Adolescent in Group and Family Therapy*, ed. M. Sugar. New York: Brunner/Mazel, pp. 87-104.

742. Spruiell, V. (1975), Adolescent Narcissism and Group Psychotherapy. In: *The Adolescent in Group and Family Therapy*, ed. M. Sugar. New York: Brunner/Mazel, pp. 27-41.

743. Sugar, M. (1975), Office Network Therapy with Adolescents. In: *The Adolescent in Group and Family Therapy*, ed. M. Sugar. New York: Brunner/Mazel, pp. 105-117.

744. Sugar, M. (1975), Group Therapy for Pubescent Boys with Absent Fathers. In: *The Adolescent in Group and Family Therapy*, ed. M. Sugar. New York: Brunner/Mazel, pp. 49-67.

745. Sugar, M. (1975), The Structure and Setting of Adolescent Therapy Groups. In: *The Adolescent in Group and Family Therapy*, ed. M. Sugar. New York: Brunner/Mazel, pp. 42-48.

746. Hurst, A., et al. (1978), Leadership Style Determinants of Cohesiveness in Adolescent Group.

*International Journal of Group Psychotherapy.*
28:263-277.

747. Weinstock, A. (1979), Group Treatment of Characterologically Damaged, Developmentally Disabled Adolescents in a Residential Treatment Center. *International Journal of Group Psychotherapy.* 29:369-381.

748. Deleted.

I. Deprived Children

749. Scheidlinger, S. (1960), Experiential Group Treatment of Severely Deprived Latency Age Children. *American Journal of Orthopsychiatry.* 30:356-368.

750. Scheidlinger, S. (1965), Three Group Approaches with Socially Deprived Latency-age Children. *International Journal of Group Psychotherapy.* 15:434-445.

751. Empey, L.T. (1968), Sociological Perspectives and Small-Group Work with Socially Deprived Youth. *Social Service Review.* 42:448-463.

752. MacLennan, B.W. (1968), Group Approaches to the Problems of Socially Deprived Youth: The Classical Psychotherapeutic Model. *International Journal of Group Psychotherapy.* 18:481-494.

753. Franklin, G., and Nottage, W. (1969), Psychoanalytic Treatment of Severely Disturbed Juvenile Delinquents in a Therapy Group. *International Journal of Group Psychotherapy.* 19:165-175.

754. Piuck, C.L. (1970), Evolution of a Treatment Method for Disadvantaged Children. *American Journal of Psychotherapy.* 24:112-123.

755. Scheidlinger, S. (1970), Therapeutic Group Approaches with Ghetto Youth. *Newsletter: American Orthopsychiatric Association.* 14:16-17.

J. The Role of Visitors in Children's Groups

756. Freeman, H., and King, C. (1957), The Role of Visitors in Activity Group Therapy. *International Journal of Group Psychotherapy.* 7:289-301.

K. Parents Groups

757. Feinstein, H.; Paul, N.; and Esmiol, P. (1964), Group Therapy for Mothers with Infanticidal Impulses. *American Journal of Psychiatry.* 120:882-886.

758. Goodman, H., and Kahn, R. (1973), Successful Adaptations of Group Therapy Techniques in the Treatment of Socially and Economically Deprived Mothers of School Children. *American Journal of Orthopsychiatry.* 43:262.

# AUTHOR INDEX

Abrahams, D., 450
Abramson, R.M., 724
Abroms, G.M., 394, 624
Adsett, C.A., 540
Aiello, T., 363
Alexander, L., 563
Alikakos, L.C., 325
Allgeyer, J.M., 472, 474
Almond, R., 351, 492, 625, 633, 634
Al Salih, H.A., 399
Altman, S., 719
Ament, A., 519
Ammon, G., 130, 519, 554
Anderson, B.N., 499
Aronson, M.D., 229
Arriaga, K., 590
Arsenian, J., 10, 92, 117, 217, 322, 516, 517,
Asch, S., 63
Ascher, E., 5
Astrachan, B.M., 71, 154, 425, 479, 492, 495, 524, 532, 580, 626
Azima, F.J., 11

Bacal, H., 565
Bailis, S.S., 591
Bales, R.G., 93
Balint, M., 564
Ball, D., 564
Banquer, M., 347
Barcai, A., 695, 717
Bartz, W.R., 675
Battegay, R., 209, 259, 650
Bayrakal, S., 555

Beal, D., 361
Beard, J., 304
Beck, J.C., 484, 487
Becker, B.J., 123
Belinkoff, J., 180
Bell, R.W., 611
Benjamin, S.E., 277
Bennett, M., 475
Benson, M., 423
Beran, M., 255, 311, 579
Berger, I.L., 493
Berger, M.M., 525, 539
Berkovitz, I., 739
Berman, L., 111
Bernandez, T., 263
Bernard, H.S., 469
Bernardez-Bonesatti, T., 574
Berne, E., 623
Bernstein, S., 190, 591
Bienlein, D.K., 674
Billings, J., 383
Bilodeau, C.B., 544
Bion, W.R., 97, 98, 424
Birk, L., 13, 150
Blau, D., 476
Blinder, M.G., 432
Bloch, H.S., 471
Bloch, S., 514
Bloom, J.D., 459
Bloom, V., 264
Bloomfield, H.H., 347
Bogdanoff, M., 293
Borenzweig, H., 414
Boris, H.N., 78
Borriello, J.F., 107
Bourguignon, O., 566
Bower, P.F., 347
Branum, M.C., 672
Bratter, T.E., 375
Brockbank, R., 118, 121
Bross, R., 180
Brown, S., 378

Brownfield, B., 310
Buck, L.A., 614
Buck, R.E., 663
Buda, B., 132
Bugh, V.G., 649
Burke, J.L., 319
Burnside, I.M., 409
Butler, B., 607

Cabral, R., 685
Carney, F.L., 391
Cartwright, D., 21
Casriel, D.H., 160
Caudill, W., 618
Chalfen, L., 201
Chance, E., 496
Cherbuliez, T., 725
Chertoff, H.R., 684
Chertok, L., 566
Chesteen, J.E., Jr., 312
Chiles, J.A., 452
Christ, J. 190, 335, 435, 731
Christmas, J.J., 334, 483
Cladwell, H.S., 553
Claghorn, J., 348
Cochrane, N., 344, 440
Cohn, R.C., 94
Committee on History, 1
Comstock, B., 352, 384
Coolidge, J., 726
Cory, T., 362, 364, 592
Costell, R.M., 23
Coughlin, F., 458
Covi, L., 226, 397
Crabtree, L.H., Jr., 401
Crowder, D.L., 735
Crutcher, R., 387
Cumming, E., 621
Cumming, J., 621
Curlee, J., 373
Curry, A.E., 657

Danesh, H.B., 238
Dang, J.C., 281
Daniels, C.R., 712
Daniels, D.N., 608
Daniels, R., 307
Dannefer, E., 722
Davies, I.J., 455
Davis, F., 276
Davis, J.A., 339
Day, M., 18, 119, 261, 300, 520
Deitch, D., 160
de Mare, P., 597
Demarest, E., 177, 267
Denny, J.M., 613
Desmond, R., 427
Detre, T.P., 479
Deutsch, A.L., 537
Dick, B.M., 686
Dickens, G., 612
Dies, R.R., 196, 689
Dobie, S.I., 264
Dolan, L.P., 377
Donovan, J., 475
Drennen, W., 320
Druck, A.B., 175, 593
Dumont, M.P., 330
Dupont, M., 265
Durkin, H.E., 3, 65, 95, 109, 156, 158, 185, 187, 647
Dyck, G., 733

Eddy, W., 170
Egan, M.H., 706
Eisner, B.G., 224
Elbaum, P., 293
Ellsworth, R., 628
Elmore, J.L., 586
Empey, L.T., 751
Enright, J.D., 450
Epstein, N., 719
Esmiol, P., 757
Esty, J.F., 523
Everett, H.C., 434
Ezriel, H., 96, 99, 101, 178

Farberow, N., 381
Farrell, J.P., 179
Feinstein, H., 757
Feldberg, T., 285
Ferone, L., 392
Fidler, G.S., 609
Fidler, J.W., 326, 635
Field, G.D., 575
Fielding, B., 202
Fischer, N., 401
Fisher, B., 501, 558
Fleischl, M., 589
Fogelman, M.A., 577
Ford, C.V., 559
Forer, B., 313
Foulkes, S.H., 62, 104, 243, 598, 664
Fox, R., 372
Frank, J.D., 5, 6, 19, 81, 393, 449, 651
Frank, M.G., 692
Frankena, S.T., 511
Franklin, G., 753
Frederick, C.J., 381
Freedman, M.B., 30
Freeman, H., 756
Freud, S., 124
Freundlich, D., 661
Frey, N.C., 345
Fried, E., 2, 183, 237, 240, 246, 250, 252, 366, 369, 573
Friedman, H., 720
Friedman, L.J., 73
Fromm-Reichmann, F., 617
Furst, W., 58

Galinsky, M., 4, 102, 106, 126, 135, 139, 145, 151, 166, 172, 173
Gans, R.W., 269, 502
Ganzarain, R., 157
Garai, J., 616
Gardner, M., 464, 578
Garland, J.A., 91
Gasdick, J.M., 143
Gauron, E.R., 53

Geis, H.J., 165
Geller, J.J., 56, 321, 503
Geller, M., 261
Gershman, H., 406
Gilder, R., 561
Ginott, H.G., 702
Glad, D.D., 12, 316
Glasser, N., 454
Glassman, S.M., 660
Glatzer, H.T., 57, 176, 184, 187, 214, 231, 368, 395, 400, 509
Glotfelty, J., 74
Godenne, G.D., 728
Gold, S.R., 694
Gold, V.J., 205
Goldberg, D.A., 500
Goldfarb, W., 698
Goldstein, S., 335
Golner, J., 217, 322
Goodman, B., 500
Goodman, H., 758
Goodman, M., 189
Goodson, M.D., 288
Gottnick, I., 353
Gottlieb, A., 431
Gottschalk, L.A., 169
Gottsegen, M.G., 736
Goulding, R., 146
Graham, F., 256
Grasso, M., 736
Gratton, L., 701
Grayson, H., 247
Greaves, C., 412
Green, R., 407
Greenbaum, H., 301
Greene, R.J., 735
Grobman, J., 28, 297, 482
Grossman, W.K., 512
Grotjahn, M., 41, 87, 125, 253, 504, 526
Gruen, W., 140, 153
Grunebaum, H., 46, 80, 134, 292, 435, 436, 687
Grunebaum, M.G., 705, 726
Gurman, A.S., 442

Gurri, J., 300
Guttmacher, J., 13, 235

Hackett, T.P., 544
Hadden, S., 403, 420
Haizlip, T., 696
Haley, J., 308
Handlon, J.H., 453
Hare, M., 564
Hare, R.T., 511
Harrow, M., 457
Haskill, E.L., 155
Hawkins, D.R., 530
Haythorn, W.W., 59
Heckel, R.V., 38, 152
Heilfron, M., 164, 274
Heitler, J.B., 52
Held, M.L., 738
Herman, S., 418
Hershelman, P., 661
Herz, M.I., 349
Hidas, G., 132
Hildreth, A.M., 529
Hoffman, J.M., 92
Hoffman, L., 724
Holden, M.A., 389
Hollingsworth, S., 652
Hollon, T.H., 547
Holt, H., 670
Hooper, E., 599
Hopper, M., 600
Hora, T., 282, 305
Horowitz, M.J., 331, 655
Horwitz, L., 45, 105, 108, 181, 291, 491, 497, 521
Hulse, W.C., 9, 306
Hunt, W., 428
Hurst, A., 29, 746

Illing, H., 310, 422
Indin, B.M., 380
Intagliata, J., 379
Issacharoff, A., 428

Jackson, J., 253
Jacobs, M.A., 731
James, S.L., 730
Jarvis, P.E., 523
Johns, C.A., 724
Johnson, D.L., 694
Johnson, M., 477
Jones, H.B., 710
Jones, H.E., 91
Jones, M.N., 352, 637, 638, 641, 642, 646, 652
Jones, W.L., 433

Kadis, A.L., 197, 212, 223, 439
Kahn, R., 758
Kamin, I., 518
Kantar, S., 117
Kanter, S.S., 230, 505, 542
Kaplan, H.I., 148, 527, 528
Kaplan, R., 90
Kaplan, S.R., 34, 206, 207, 522
Karmiol, E., 512
Karson, S., 713
Kass, D.J., 394
Kassau, M., 138
Kassoff, A., 268, 727
Kates, W., 46
Kauff, P.F., 222
Kaye, H., 278
Kelman, H., 7, 682
Kernberg, P.F., 327, 654
Kew, C.E., 278
Kibel, H.D., 294, 336, 382, 594
Kilgo, R.D., 443
King, C.H., 309, 697, 756
Kirby, K., 302, 429
Kirschenbaum, M., 432
Klapman, J.W., 174, 669
Klein, F.M., 426
Klein, R.H., 469
Klein-Lipshutz, E., 199
Knoepfel, H., 567
Kogan, W.S., 70
Kohn, R., 438

Kolodny, R.L., 91
Koran, L.M., 23
Kornhaber, A., 541
Kraft, I.A., 693, 732, 737
Kramer, A., 614
Kramer, H., 303
Kramer, M., 307
Kramish, A., 606
Krasner, J.D., 262, 411
Kraus, R.F., 338
Krieger, M.H., 70
Krumboltz, J.D., 25
Kymissis, P., 615

Laffel, J., 668
Lakin, M., 75, 494
Lamberd, W.G., 656
Lambert, S.R., 591
Lane, D.M., 553
Lanning, W.L., 510
Lansky, R., 463
Larson, V.B., 451
Lassiter, R.E., 548
Laufer, L., 558
Lazarus, A.A., 398
Lazarus, H.R., 674
Leal, M.R.M., 715
Lee, H., 319
Lehrer-Carle, I., 340, 678
Leichter, E., 441, 444, 460
Leopold, H.S., 32, 35, 213, 588
LeVay, M., 709
Leveque, K.I., 553
Levin, E.C., 456
Levin, S., 8, 505
Levine, C.O., 281
Lewis, B.F., 88
Lewis, D.J., 629
Lewis, J.C., 454
Liberman, R.P., 22, 149, 357
Lieberman, F., 699
Lieberman, M.A., 68, 72, 75, 103, 494
Liederman, P.C., 407, 408

Lifton, N., 700
Limenatani, D., 261
Lindsay, J.S.B., 61
Lindt, H., 211
Lippit, D.L., 464, 578
Lippman, A., 537
Litman, R.E., 402
Lloyd, G., 473
Lofgren, L.B., 358
Lohr, N.E., 276
Long, K.D., 559
Lothenstein, L.M., 55
Low, M., 445
Low, P., 445
Luber, R.F., 461
Lubin, B., 170
Lucas, D., 241
Ludwig, A.M., 359
Ludwik, M.S., 241

Mack, J., 653, 672
MacLennan, B.W., 271, 498, 707, 752
MacLeod, J., 315
Magazu, P., 217, 322
Main, T., 568, 601, 665
Malan, D.H., 688
Mally, M., 289
Manaster, A., 410
Mann, J., 64, 298
Mann, W., 549
Markowitz, M., 197, 439
Marks, M., 189
Marohn, R.C., 627, 658
Masnick, R., 341
Matkon, A., 659
Mattison, S., 280
Maxmen, J.S., 14, 468, 587, 595
May, P.R.A., 360
McDermott, M., 384
McElroy, C., 475
McGee, T.F., 50, 220, 221, 275, 328, 342, 451, 478, 480, 507
Meltzer, H.Y., 85

Menninger, R.W., 535
Mickow, G., 423
Middleman, F., 315
Miles, J.E., 422
Miller, P.R., 392
Mintz, E.E., 137, 144, 198, 257, 270, 272, 404, 508, 515
Mitscherlich, A., 596
Moadel, Y., 583
Mone, L.C., 543
Moreau, A., 569
Moreno, J.L., 141
Morrice, J.K.W., 622
Morris, J.D., 446
Morse, S., 570
Mullan, H., 36, 48, 136
Munzer, J., 242
Murphy, A., 550
Musto, D.F., 532

Neighbor, J.E., 33
Neto, B., 192
Niver, E.O., 671
Nobler, H., 405
Nottage, W., 753

O'Brien, C., 343, 354
Ogston, W., 289
O'Hearne, J.J., 12, 147
Ohlmeier, D., 551
Oradei, D.M., 556
Ormont, L.R., 47, 193, 232, 234, 244

Page, D., 362, 364, 592
Papanek, H., 215, 251, 533
Parloff, M.B., 69, 120, 162, 449, 453, 682, 684, 691
Pattison, E.M., 169, 431, 488, 545, 581
Paul, N.L., 459, 757
Payn, S.B., 225, 227, 329, 350
Payne, J., 415
Peck, H.B., 448, 485
Peck, M., 704
Pelosi, A.A., 720

Peters, C., 292
Peters, J.J., 421
Pine, I., 464, 578
Pines, M., 290
Pinney, E.L., 39, 501
Piper, W.E., 690
Piuck, C.L., 754
Pizzitola, D., 345
Podnos, B., 506
Powdermaker, F.B., 113, 393
Prescott, M.R., 446
Priestman, S., 302, 429
Prosen, H., 656
Pyrke, M., 287, 367

Rabin, H.M., 51, 273
Rachman, A.W., 734
Racusen, F., 220, 478, 480
Radin, S.S., 698
Rahe, H., 552
Rand, K., 20
Rappaport, R.G., 390, 638
Rashkis, H.A., 639
Raskin, D.E., 643
Rathod, N.H., 709
Rawlings, E.I., 53
Reckless, J., 437, 546
Redl, F., 691
Redlich, F.C., 495, 524
Resnick, H.L.P., 421
Resnik, S., 317
Rice, A.K., 76
Richmond, A.H., 585
Riess, B.F., 610
Rioch, D.M., 619
Rioch, M., 100, 534, 536
Rizzo, A.E., 701, 740
Robbins, E., 333
Roberts, J.P., 560
Robinson, E.H., 717
Robinson, L.D., 419
Robinson, L.H., 416, 506
Rockberger, H., 189

Roether, H.A., 24
Rogers, C., 159, 161
Roman, M., 34
Rose, S., 576
Rosen, S., 138
Rosenbaum, M., 36, 48, 539
Rosenberg, J., 725
Rosenhan, D.L., 644
Rostov, B.W., 645
Roth, B.E., 295, 370
Roth, S., 258
Rueveni, V., 337

Sadock, B.J., 148, 466, 527, 528, 729
Sadoff, R.L., 42, 218
Sager, C., 254
Salzberg, H., 152
Sands, P.M., 374
Sarason, I., 668
Saravay, S.M., 129
Saretsky, T., 171
Saunders, R., 586
Savran, B., 577
Saxon, L., 740
Schamess, G., 723
Schechter, S., 280
Scheidlinger, S., 82, 83, 84, 86, 115, 122, 287, 367, 389, 485, 486, 703, 711, 714, 716, 749, 750, 755
Scher, M., 477, 481
Schiff, S.B., 660
Schinke, S., 576
Schneider, C., 60
Schulman, G.L., 460
Schuman, B.N., 220, 275
Schwartz, E.K., 67, 200, 396
Schwartz, M., 620, 636
Sedlmair, M., 679
Seligman, M., 427
Selvini, A., 572
Semrad, E.V., 10, 117, 119, 298, 299, 300, 516, 517
Shabert, J., 563
Shader, R.I., 85
Shafar, S., 43

Shaffer, J., 4, 102, 106, 126, 135, 139, 145, 151, 166, 172, 173
Shambaugh, P.W., 542
Shapiro, D., 117
Shapiro, R., 741
Sharpe, M., 612
Shaskan, D.A., 283
Shattan, S., 332
Sheps, J., 323
Sherman, M.A., 211
Sherman, R.W., 529
Shiffer, M., 708
Shrader, W.K., 467
Simkin, J.S., 204
Singer, D.L., 79
Singler, J.R., 557
Sisley, E., 679
Skynner, A.C.R., 602, 666
Slagle, S., 585
Slavinska-Holy, N., 355
Slavson, S.R., 31, 66, 114, 116, 186, 314, 582
Slawson, P.F., 538
Slivkin, S.E., 676
Smolen, E.M., 700
Snow, D.L., 738
Solomon, C.K., 142
Solomon, E., 15
Solomon, L.F., 80, 134
Solomon, M.L., 142
Speck, R., 337
Spiegal, D., 413
Spitz, H.I., 447
Spotnitz, H., 194, 233, 284, 531
Springmann, R., 603, 662
Spruiell, V., 742
Standish, C.T., 299, 300
Stannard, D.L., 632
Stanton, A.H., 619, 636
Stauble, W.J., 630
Steffens, E., 677
Stein, A., 37, 180, 182, 228, 648
Steiner, J., 346, 365, 680
Stewart, R., 704

Stock, D., 68, 103
Stone, A.R., 449
Stone, W.N., 89, 239, 266
Stotsky, B.A., 318
Strassberg, D., 356
Strauss, J., 279
Strelnick, A.H., 462
Strunk, C., 721
Stubblebine, J.M., 640
Suarez, R., 386
Sugar, M., 739, 743, 744, 745
Sweet, B.S., 30

Tavormina, J.B., 417
Taylor, S.S., 699
Teicher, A., 167, 177, 267
Toker, E., 210
Towey, M.R., 673
Trakas, D.A., 473
Tredgold, R., 571
Turquet, P., 604, 667

Udelman, D., 562
Udelman, H., 562

Van Putten, T., 360
Vass, I., 388
Vick, J.W., 737
Volkan, V.D., 530
Von Scoy, H., 718

Wacks, J., 190, 191
Waite, N.S., 556
Wallace, A.F.C., 639
Wallace, E.R., 27, 131
Waxer, P.H., 470
Weich, M.J., 333
Weiner, M.F., 195, 245
Weinstock, A., 747
Weisberg, P., 331, 655
Weisselberger, D., 236
Wells, R.A., 461
Wells, S.H., 501

Wentworth-Rohr, I., 77
Wermers, D.F., 385
Westman, J.C., 430
Weyman, A., 600
Whitaker, D., 75, 494
White, N.L., 631
Whiteley, J.S., 605
Whitman, R.M., 89, 103, 208, 239
Wiggins, S., 320
Willett, A.B., 548
Williams, M., 342, 415, 489
Williams, R.L., 143
Wimberger, H.C., 458
Winick, C., 223, 670
Wise, M., 385
Witkin, L.J., 721
Wolf, A., 67, 110, 112, 127, 200, 465
Wolff, H., 15
Wolff, R.A., 681
Wolman, B.B., 286
Wong, N., 260, 296, 324, 371

Yalom, I.D., 16, 17, 20, 26, 40, 44, 49, 54, 128, 133, 163, 168, 188, 216, 248, 249, 376, 378, 412, 413, 490, 683
Yano, B., 563

Zilbach, J., 476, 692, 705
Zimet, C.N., 60
Zimmerman, D., 203, 219
Zinberg, N.E., 73, 74
Zolik, E.S., 318

## SUBJECT INDEX

Acting-in, concept of in group psychotherapy, 234
Acting-out in group psychotherapy, 229, 236, 319
Activities in group therapy, 606-616
Activity group therapy, 668-681
Adolescent groups, 555, 583, 727-748
Adolescent groups, co-therapy for, 727, 728
Adolescent groups for delinquents, 727, 730, 731
Adolescent groups, in-patient, 729, 740, 747
Adolescent groups for obese females, 738
After-care groups, 476-482
Aggression in therapy groups, 24, 233, 238
Alcoholic patients, group therapy of, 372-379
Alternate sessions in group psychotherapy, 211, 212
Alumni Groups, 478, 480
Anaclitic Transference, concept of, in group psychotherapy, 180
Analytic Group Psychotherapy (see Psychoanalytic approach to groups)
Assertiveness groups, 575, 576
Asthmatic patients, group therapy of, 546

"Balint" groups, 564-572
Basic concepts in group psychotherapy, 2
Beginning group therapists, 489, 490, 505
Behavioral approach to group psychotherapy, 148-153
Blind patients, group therapy of, 418
Borderline patients, group therapy of, 282-297

Character, concept and problems in group psychotherapy, 235
Character disorders, group therapy of, 387-391
Children's groups, 691-756
Children's groups, activity group therapy, 702-708, 718-722, 724

Children's groups, adolescents, 555, 583, 727-748
Children's groups, adolescents, co-therapy for, 727, 728
Children's groups, adolescents, delinquent, 727, 730, 731, 747, 753
Children's groups, adolescents, inpatient, 729, 740, 747
Children's groups, adolescents, obese female, 738
Children's groups, combined individual and group therapy, 699, 726
Children's groups, concurrent treatment of parents and children, 709, 710
Children's groups for deprived children, 749-755
Children's groups, general issues, 691-695
Children's groups, in-patient, 724, 725
Children's groups, latency age, 711-725, 726
Children's groups, latency age, who are severely deprived, 711, 714
Children's groups, psychotic children, 697-701
Children's groups, under-achieving children, 695
Children's groups, visitors to, 756
Children's groups, young children, 696
Chronic lung disease patients, group therapy of, 545
Combined individual and group psychotherapy, 250-260
Community mental health, group therapy in, 483-488
Community psychiatry, group therapy in, 483-488
Compatibility in therapy groups, 20, 23
Composition of therapy groups, 54, 57-59
Confrontation in group psychotherapy, 246
Corrective emotional experience in group psychotherapy, 5
Co-therapy, male and female, use of, in group psychotherapy, 272
Co-therapy, use of, in group psychotherapy, 267-281, 661
Co-therapy, use of, in training therapists, 499, 502
Crisis-oriented group therapy, 471-475
Countertransference in group psychotherapy, 189-198, 244
Countertransference, use of, in group supervision, 198
Couples, group psychotherapy of, 429-447
Curative factors in group psychotherapy, 5-17, 30

Deaf patients, group psychotherapy of, 419
Demonstration groups, 531

Depressed patients, group psychotherapy of, 392
Developmental stages in social work groups, 91
Developmental stages in therapy groups, 90, 216
Diagnostic groups, 448
Didactic group psychotherapy, 174, 175, 467
Doctors, groups for, 564-572
Dreams in group psychotherapy, 199-209
Drop-outs from group psychotherapy, 38, 40, 41, 55
Dying patients, group psychotherapy of, 412, 413

Empathy, concept of, in group psychotherapy, 83
Encounter groups, 159-168
Exhibitionism in group psychotherapy, 231
Existential-Experiential approach to groups, 135, 136

Family group therapy, 453-463
Fees in group psychotherapy, 223
Freudian group psychology and group psychotherapy, 115, 116, 124, 128, 131

Genital issues in group psychotherapy, 230
Geriatric patients, group psychotherapy of, 407-411
Gestalt approach to group psychotherapy, 137-140, 204
Group-as-a-Whole approach to groups, 96-108
Group-centered approach to groups, 96-108
Group cohesiveness, 18-29
Group dreams, 206, 208, 209
Group dynamic approach to groups, 103-108
Group dynamics, 62-89
Group dynamics, aggression, 596
Group dynamics, boundary management in, 79
Group dynamics, "group-as-a-whole" phenomena, 68, 72
Group dynamics, identity issues in large groups, 604
Group dynamics, intergroup processes, 76
Group dynamics in large groups, 601
Group dynamics, patterns in early group meetings, 81
Group dyanmics, peer interaction, 74, 80
Group dynamics, social pressure, 63
Group dynamics, training in, 493, 495, 516, 517, 519
Group process, 62-89
Group relations, 532-536
Group silences, 88
Group therapy compared with individual therapy, 8, 15, 43

Heart attack patients, group psychotherapy of, 540, 543, 544, 551, 552, 558
Help-rejecting complainers, group psychotherapy of, 292, 539
Hemodialysis patients, group psychotherapy of, 542, 547
Hemophiliac patients, group psychotherapy of, 533
History of group therapy, 1, 3, 4
Holocaust survivors, group psychotherapy of, 577
Homosexual patients, group psychotherapy of, 257, 402-406
Homosexual patients, male, group psychotherapy of, 257

Identification, concept of, in group therapy, 82
Indications for group psychotherapy, 37, 39, 45
Individuation, concept of, in group psychotherapy, 240
In-patient groups, 578-595
Intake groups, 450, 452
Interpersonal-interactional approach to groups, 132, 133
Interpretation, use of, in group psychotherapy, 243

Laboratory training model of groups, 169-172
Large groups, 596-605, 652-667
Leaderless groups, 424-428
Learning group psychotherapy, 489-501

Marathon groups, 160
Masochistic patients, group psychotherapy for, 400-401
Medically ill patients, group psychotherapy for, 537-563
Medical students, groups for, 564-572
Medication, use of, in group psychotherapy, 224-227
Medication, use of, in group psychotherapy of chronic psychotic patients, 225, 227
Milieu therapy groups, large, 652-667
Milieu therapy groups, small, 668-661
Mood music, use of, in group psychotherapy, 241
"Mother Group," concept of, in group psychotherapy, 86

Narcissistic patients, group psychotherapy of, 252, 260, 366, 371
Neurotic patients, group psychotherapy of, 393-397
New group members, introduction of, into therapy groups, 34, 35

Obesity, group psychotherapy for, 538, 541, 548, 563
Object relations theory, application to group psychotherapy, 157
Observers, use of, in group psychotherapy, 230, 253
Oral issues, concept of, in group psychotherapy, 230, 253
Outcome studies in group psychotherapy, 682-690

Parents groups, 550, 561, 709, 710, 757, 758
Passive patients, group psychotherapy of, 252
Peer theory of groups and group psychotherapy, 134
Phobic patients, group psychotherapy of, 398-399
Preparation of lower-class patients for group psychotherapy, 52
Preparation of patients for group psychoanalysis, 47
Preparation of patients for group psychotherapy, 47-55
Post-hospitalization groups, 476-482
Psychoanalytic approach to groups, 109-131, 132, 144, 150, 200, 201, 211, 214
Psychodrama, 141-145
Psychosomatic patient groups, 537, 554, 559, 560
Psychotic patients, group psychotherapy of, 298-365

Recorders, use of, in psychotherapy groups, 261-266
Referral of patients for group psychotherapy, 30-46
Regression, concept of, in group psychotherapy, 84
Research in group psychotherapy, 682-690
Resistance in group psychotherapy, 189, 193, 232
Retarded patients, group psychotherapy of, 414-417
Rheumatoid arthritic patients, group psychotherapy of, 562

Scapegoating in group psychotherapy, 210
Schizoid patients, group psychotherapy of, 385, 386
Selection of patients for group psychotherapy, 30-46
Self-psychology, concept of, in group process and group psychotherapy, 89, 237, 239
Sexual dysfunction, group psychotherapy of, 420
Sexual offenders, group psychotherapy of, 421-423
Short-term group therapy, 464, 470
Size of therapy groups, 56, 60, 61
Socially disadvantaged patients, group psychotherapy of, 483-488

Social work approach to groups, 173
Spinal cord injured patients, group psychotherapy of, 549
Stroke patients, group psychotherapy of, 556, 557
"Study" groups (see Tavistock groups; Group relations)
Suicidal patients, group psychotherapy of, 380-384
Superego, concept of, in group psychotherapy, 228
Supervision of group psychotherapy, 502-515
Supervision of group psychotherapy, peer group, 511
Systems approach to group psychotherapy, 154-158

Tavistock groups, 96-102
Termination in group psychotherapy, 217-222
Termination in group psychotherapy, its relationship to separation-individuation, 222
Termination of individual group members, 219
Termination of therapists from psychotherapy groups, 217, 218, 221, 330
"T" groups, 169, 172
Theoretical models in group psychotherapy, 92-175
Therapeutic contract in group psychotherapy, 232, 234
Therapeutic milieu, general issues, 617-635
Therapeutic milieu, group therapy in, 645-681
Therapeutic milieu vs. therapeutic community, 636, 644
Therapeutic models in group psychotherapy, 92-175
Time-limited groups, 464-470
Training groups, 516-531
Training groups compared to therapy groups, 522
Training groups for psychiatric residents, 518, 521, 524, 527-529
Training groups, leadership in, 524
Training group therapists, 491, 492, 494, 495, 497-501
Transactional Analysis approach to groups, 146, 147
Transference and therapist transparency in group psychotherapy, 188, 195, 196
Transference in group therapy, 176-188, 267
Transference in training groups, 181
Transference neurosis in group psychotherapy, 186, 187
Transference resistance in group psychotherapy, 176

Voyeurism in group psychotherapy, 231

Waiting list groups, 451
Ward meetings, 653, 656, 658, 659
Warm-up procedures in group psychotherapy, 242
Women's groups, 573, 574
Working through in group psychotherapy, 213-216
Written summary, use of, in group psychotherapy, 248